BARBERSHOP TALES

BARBERSHOP TALES

Premiere Edition

MUSIC AND LYRICS BY:	JACOB FJELDHEIM
SCRIPT BY:	TYLER KERSTETTER
	JACKSON SMITH
EDITED BY:	CASEY DORAN

CORRUPTED AMISH PUBLISHING
MERRITT ISLAND, FL

ISBN-13: 978-0-9905663-0-4
Corrupted Amish Publishing
Merritt Island, FL
corruptedamish.us

First Printing: July, 2014
This Printing: July 2014
First edition.
1 3 5 7 9 10 8 6 4 2

TABLE OF CONTENTS

ACKNOWLEDGEMENTS

No great work exists in a vacuum, and even this script would not exist without a lot of external assistance.

On origins, we owe a lot to Ken Winn and the staff at Edgewood Jr./Sr. High School of Choice for the culture of excellence they built. In particular, Jeff Worcester provided excellent criticism of an early draft, even if he couldn't hear the music. Melanie Hale's TV production class saw the earliest version of our idea, even if it was just a gag in a short film about bad movie ideas.

The entire Edgewood Harlequins family have nourished this concept at one point or another. We proudly represent troupe 6616.

Translating a script from page to stage takes a huge leap of faith; to the Eastside High School drama program we owe much. Tammy Meyers fought for, believed in, and fostered this show from near nothing to a successful and beloved production. To them, there are too many thanks to send than can fit on this page. So, to all, thanks for jumping off with us.

We could not have gotten this script out the door without the love and support of our siblings, parents, and closest friends. Marena, Coral, Dave, and Mary Smith; Caroline, Kristin, Brittney, Richard, and Karri Fjeldheim; Tara, Taylor, Ken, and Danella Kerstetter; Kattie, Amy, John, and Sharon Doran; Jake Wade: We owe it all to you.

PREFACE

The tale of Barbershop Tales is for us, much like the show for Joel, our own coming of age tale. Since the concept was first pitched, by my count, eight girlfriends have come and gone among us, nine jobs have been loved and lost, twenty four hundred Steam and Xbox achievements have been unlocked, and all of us have both graduated from high school and taken significant steps in our personal postsecondary careers. I've been fortunate enough to see it grow and change from a joke in a homework assignment to a complex, lovingly assembled work of art.

It's hard to nail the origin of the idea to one particular day, but I think it can be reasonably narrowed. Edgewood Jr./Sr. High School of Choice in Merritt Island, Florida, is really an incredible institution. It may be pride in my origins showing through, but no matter how much I hear from my peers about the great (and terrible) educations they got, I don't hear of a single equal to Edgewood, particularly in their cultivation of students' love for learning, zeal for the act of creation, and culture of excellence- as in the school's motto- in who these students are, what they know, and what they do.

It was in an Edgewood classroom that I first heard of Barbershop Tales- Alan Clark's Honors Economics, actually. Tyler Kerstetter had been on a kick of writing sitcom pilots of late, no doubt inspired by the fun we'd been having in Melanie Hale's TV Production course. The students in that section of Econ were a potent group- Tyler kicking off ridiculous ideas, which were fed on, amplified, and (to Mr. Clark's chagrin) explicated on to the point of absurdity by myself, Megan Abbott, John Waters, and a few others.

There were dozens of them- we had a *Caddyshack* inspired golf pilot, a tale of a misfit spies, an office comedy, and, on this particular day, a show about the second oldest profession. "Barbering," Tyler would confidently assert. Another of us would say: "Yeah. And it's a musical. Full of 80's synth pop." "But there's no conflict there. What does the Barber have to choose?" "He secretly wants to design women's eveningwear, and he doesn't know how to tell his dad."

In a flash of brilliant BS, we had the makings of a story that would grip our hearts for years to come.

The next time the idea came up, we were struggling through an assignment to cap off the fall semester in Ms. Hale's TV class. We assembled what Ms. Hale then, and I to this day, refer to as the Dream Team.

Waters and Kerstetter on preproduction came up with a brilliant concept: reuse these ridiculous ideas in a short film about people pitching ridiculous film ideas to an exasperated studio executive, which was itself a writing exercise by a pair of writers- a script about people writing a script about people pitching scripts. Scriptception.

John, myself, and Johann Garces would handle the actual production in our assorted neighborhoods and the Cocoa Village area.

An Indiana Jones-esque action movie, with myself as the unintentionally dorky hero, was shot in the old Georgiana graveyard. A romantic comedy about a girl (played by Casey Madden), who meets a boy that has cats where his feet should be (played by Tyler Kerstetter). A suspenseful interrogation sequence between two all-american heroes (Kerstetter and Wyatt Garland) and a Russian spy (Madden), coining the brilliant quip "Looks like you're red on the inside too, commie."

And, there, in the middle, a musical about a boy who must choose between his barber upbringing and his dream of dressmaking. Jake Wade played Joel in this early incarnation, standing in the middle of the street outside Rick's Barber Shop in Cocoa Village, an apron we borrowed from his mother on his frame, with symbolic shears in one hand and one of Casey Madden's slinkiest dresses in the other. It was brilliant. It was inspired. It was 30 seconds long.[1]

The show got filed away for a time, well outside my sight, with little movement. Shortly before our graduation, Tyler approached resident mathemusician Jacob Fjeldheim to run some ideas for show structure. Jackson Smith, our longtime friend and an Edgewood alum, joined the meeting, and from what I gather, they decided that that summer of 2011 would be the summer they write a full length stage musical based on that idea.

---

[1] The video, Pitch, is still online as of this writing, on the YouTube channel youtube.com/videoontheedge

They shared with me a Google Drive folder filled with notes, lyrics, bits of dialogue, and descriptions of sets in a state that can only be described as disarray. I didn't contribute much then- I never counted myself as a writer or musician- but it was cool to see our idea take shape. The barbershop had been in the family for generations. Joel was pulled from his path not by his own desire to run a dress shop, but by a love interest named Judy. The population of Birchwood grew and diversified.

Summer ended. We went our separate ways (Jackson, to UCF for a creative writing degree; Jacob, to UF to study what he referred to as "neurophysics"; Tyler to join the Army; myself to Florida Tech to study computer science), promising to come back to this idea at some point in the future. I became buried in my work, and for me, Barbershop Tales was once again a joke that we could use to impress girls or annoy people in theatrical circles.

A Facebook group formed at some point that year, Barbershop Tales Fanclub. Jackson and Jacob and Tyler would occasionally post interesting tidbits about the show, but from the inside it looked like they were just teasing a bunch of old high school friends.

The next summer, of 2012, was a busy one. Jackson and Wyatt Garland started a webcomic entitled Down Right Radical[2], Tyler was traveling all over the nation for training, and Jacob was (to my knowledge) working in theaters in Gainesville. History became legend. Legend became myth. And for a time, the state of Barbershop Tales passed out of all my knowledge. Until…

One day, towards the end of that summer or early in the school year that followed, Jacob posted a link to a Soundcloud playlist containing 5 songs from the show, played on piano and ukulele, sung by himself and Jackson, to the fanclub[3]. He followed with a bonus track from Toy Story, and, later, another track: Starting to Feel Something.

---

[2] Now semipermanently on hiatus. You can check out the archives at downrightradical.com

[3] soundcloud.com/jacobfjeldheim/sets/barbershop-tales-demos

Barbershop Tales was alive and well. The three collaborated remotely for a while, building out the script and getting outside review, including a very helpful set of notes from our AP English teacher at Edgewood, Jeff Worcester. And, just when I thought BST fever couldn't get any higher, someone new posted to the fanclub: Tammy Meyers. Her link was simple, but for us life changing: A Facebook event, inviting us out to see the show performed live for the very first time at Eastside High School in Gainesville.

Shortly thereafter I started to tap back into the backend of BST development, assembling a master script from the various Google Docs and applying proper formatting, reaching out to Jacob while he directed the show at EHS to get things like license agreements filled and copyrights applied for. When the opening week rolled around, Tyler, myself, and my girlfriend made the long trip up to Gainesville to see Jacob and the EHS cast put on a show that brought tears of joy to our eyes. Even my girlfriend, numb to my own antics, remarked "This is a really, really ridiculously good show." I later found a jazz album by Jacob on her iPod.

I kept on formatting and refining the script, now transferred from Google Docs to the more print-friendly Microsoft Word, throughout the summer. When I got an email from Tammy by way of Jacob asking if we could publish the show so that students could perform parts from it in competitions, I was more than ready. A week of frenzied assembly resulted in this, the premiere edition of Barbershop Tales, in print.

I'd be remiss if I failed to make the following note: This is not the final edition of this script. Far from it, in fact. This is a snapshot of the script that was put on at EHS, but we received so much excellent feedback from Tammy and the audience that we're already planning some big changes, particularly to explicate on the fate of Judy[4], in future editions.

---

4 When applying for copyright, we listed "Judy Dies" as an alternate title. We've always known that our handling of that part needed some love.

If you come by this script and are interested in performing it (or even just want Jacob's music to review), feel free to contact us. We can be reached at corruptedamish@gmail.com.

Many resources are available to licensed performers, including recordings, DRM-free sheet music, marketing materials, a network of other organizations that have performed this show, and additional show promotion services. This is the first of hopefully many books and products by Corrupted Amish publishing. You can always find the latest info about our content at our site, corruptedamish.us.

It's been an honor getting from there to here. I can't wait to see where we go from here.

-Casey Doran

DEBUT CAST

Barbershop Tales debuted at Eastside High School in Gainesville, Florida, on April 17, 2014, at 7 PM.

Cast:

Gaby (Bubba, gender-bent) - Gabrielle Gaither
Joel - Kyle Tapley
Bill - Patric Mann
Timmy - Terrence Williams
Judy - Brittany Bennett
David/Daphne - Dominick Aslanian & Laura Clark
Alex - Mariam Mohamed
Carol/Fabulous She-Vagrant - Morgan Worthy
Ellie - Brittany Fletcher & Sophie Clark
Rachel - Dayo Nunn
Olsen - Benjamin Morris
Charlie - Aliya Miranda
Mac/Patron - Mark Colandreo
Jenny/Patron/Fabulous She-Vargrant - Vivian El-Salaway
Gary/Patron/Vagrant - Xavier Crawford
Fabulous She-Vagrant/Townie - Jordan Fulkerson
Vagrant/Townie - Micaela Cuneo
Vagrant/Townie - Skye Melrose
Fabulous Trash Can Vagrant - Stephon Jaminson
Police/Doctors - Jordan Capeloto, Xavier Crawford, Drew Doerr, Jacob Fjeldheim

Crew:

Director - Jacob Fjeldheim
Student Director - Braxton Thompson
Student Director - Derek Jarvis
Producer - Tammy Meyers
Stage Manager - Maria McNieve
Assistant Stage Manager - Jasmine Jackson
Lighting - Ty Holder, Benjamin Brandt
Sound - Antonio Romero, Chance Rowan, Summer Melrose
Costume Designer - Bridget Whiting
Assistant Costume Designer - Sylmacia Hall
Spotlight Operator - Jarling Liu, Rachel Cohan
Piano - Jacob Fjeldheim
Bass - Nate Garland
Drums - Jonathan Foster

SETS

Barbershop Tales was written with limited set requirements in mind, but a few considerations need be made:

There should be a lit barber pole on stage at most times. This pole should be controlled from the lighting system, for effect.

The barbershop set should be on stage at all times. This can be a simple set: a few chairs, a counter, and wall decorations. We suggest it be raised from stage height, not more than would be by a platform of two by fours. This set will also hold the wall-mounted family shears.

There should be a static "park" set, consisting of a bench and climbable tree. Backdrop for this part should evoke a small town, main street vibe. We use assorted storefronts.

The various vagrants may elect to occupy the front row of the theater. If possible, they may wish to make themselves a home, with cardboard, trash barrels, oil drum fires, blankets, etc. The juxtaposition between vagrants below and white picket fence small town above is not accidental.

CHARACTERS

Bubba - A wise homeless person.
Joel - The protagonist. A barber by trade.
Judy - Joel's love interest, a kind homeless person.
Timmy - Joel's best friend. A jobless, introspective soul.
Bill - Joel's father, proprietor of the barbershop.
Charlie - Timmy's love interest, an employee of Bill's shop.
Ellie - An employee of Bill's shop.
Rachel - An employee of Bill's shop.
Mac - Bill's friend, a regular patron of the shop.
Alex - A homeless person.
David - A homeless person.
Carol - A homeless person.
Olsen- One of Bill's poker buddies.
Jenny- One of Bill's poker buddies.
Gary- One of Bill's poker buddies.
Assorted police, doctors, vagrants, townies, and patrons.

ACT ONE, SCENE 1

1. PROLOGUE

An old timey tune wafts through the air; spotlight on a man sitting on a black stool. He wears a black suit and skinny tie, a classy black fedora and black sunglasses. He's a cat who's been around the block a few times and he's sung his share of the blues. This is BUBBA.

BUBBA

Well hello there folks. So nice of you to join us out here tonight. Ol' Bubba's got quite a story for you, if you've got the time to listen. It's a tale of love and family, of coming of age and responsibility... but mostly it's a tale about a barbershop. We might as well start right at the beginning... but if I'm gonna tell this story, I'm gonna need a little help. Gimme a hand here girls!

Curtain comes up on a TRIO of girls standing in front of the lowered scrim. They all wear white pants, red and white striped shirts, and flat straw hats.

BUBBA (CONT'D)

NOW HERE'S THE STORY OF A MAN CALLED JOEL
AND THE BARBERSHOP O'ER WHICH HE'S GONNA TAKE CONTROL
AND SO, BOYS AND GIRLS, LET'S TAKE A STROLL
ON THESE LONG AND WINDING TRAILS
BILL IS HIS FATHER, JOEL CALLS HIM POP
AND BILL, HE'S READY FOR SON TO TAKE THE SHOP
BUT A LITTLE GAL JUDY'S GONNA MAKE THAT STOP
AND SO GO THE BARBERSHOP TALES

BUBBA (CONT'D)
(Out of rhythm.)

Yessum, that shop has been around near past a century by now, and every owner has earned his place in Birchwood's history and, in turn, passed that legacy on to his son. That's just the way it's been 'round these parts; father to son, barber to barber, never a break in the barbershop tales. But for how long that will continue...well let's just say that's up to young Joel now...girls, show 'em around.

BARBER TRIO

JOEL'S CUTTIN
TIMMY'S STRUTTIN
BILL'S EXCHANGING
JOEL IS CHANGING
BILL IS URGING
PAST'S RESURGING
NOW (NOW) (NOW) (NOW) (NOW)
BILL'S KNOWIN
JUDY'S SEWIN
JOEL'S GROWIN
JUDY'S SHOWIN
TIMMY'S SHOVIN
JOEL IS LOVIN
WHAT WILL BILL ALLOW?

> Transforms into rock, blows straight into BARBERSHOP
> TALES.

ACT ONE, SCENE 2

It's mid-morning and there is hustle and bustle around downtown Birchwood. Inside the shop is BILL along with the barbershop trio from the prologue, ELLIE, RACHEL, and CHARLIE. BILL is a strong-jawed man is in his mid-40s and wears beige slacks with a simple white button up. The BARBER TRIO and BILL are in the process of opening up the shop. BILL opens the door to the back room and goes in just as JOEL enters stage left. JOEL is a bright-eyed and bushy-tailed twenty year old. He comes running across the stage into MAC, a pedestrian.

MAC
Whoa there!

JOEL
Ah! Sorry Mac, late for work, can't talk!

MAC
(Jokingly.)
Why am I not surprised?

JOEL brushes past MAC and enters the shop.

JOEL
Morning ladies!

BARBER TRIO
Morning Joel!

JOEL takes off his jacket and switches on the spinning barber pole. BILL comes out of the back room, JOEL does not see him.

BILL
(Laughing.)
Some things just never change.

JOEL
(Startled at first.)
Way to warn me! You nearly gave me a heart attack, pop!

BILL grins and tosses an apron to JOEL as JOEL tosses BILL his jacket. JOEL grabs a broom but BILL takes it from him.

BILL
So how about we get this show on the road?

JOEL
I'd like nothing more!

2. BARBERSHOP TALES

JOEL (CONT'D)
GOOD MORNING MONDAY, MY FAVORITE TIME
THE DAY THAT STARTS OFF EVERY WEEK
THE FAMILY BIZ, THIS OLD HOME OF MINE

The BARBER TRIO enters the barbershop via a back door as customers come in for a haircut or shave.

BARBER TRIO
VERY BOLD, CLASSIC, AND UNIQUE!

JOEL
EVERY MORNING, EIGHT O'CLOCK
WE OPEN SAME TIME EVERY DAY
SOME PEOPLE COME BY TO HEAR US SING
AND OTHER GUYS DECIDE TO STAY
ALL THIS CUTTING
ALL THIS SHAVING
FEELS SO RIGHT TO ME
I WANNA SAY POP, I'M LOVING LIVING
IN MY BARBER FAMILY

BARBER TRIO
COME DROP BY THE BARBERSHOP
YOU GOTTA HOP HOP HOP TO THE BARBERSHOP
YOU BETTER STOP STOP STOP BY THE BARBERSHOP
YOU BETTER COME BY OUR WAY EVERY DAY!

4

JOEL

EVERY DAY PEOPLE ON THE STREET
GO THROUGH THE SAME OLD DULL ROUTINE
YOU SEE 'EM WALKING, YOU SEE 'EM TALKING
SAD

GIRLS

GLOOMY!

JOEL

DOWN AND MEAN
THEY GO TO WORK
THEY GO TO SCHOOL
PRAYIN' SOMEONE MISBEHAVES
BUT WE PROVIDE WHAT THEY REALLY NEED
SOME SHORT CLIPPERS AND A SHAVE
I LOVE CLIPPIN'
RAZOR GRIPPIN'
STARTS MY DAY OUT RIGHT
I'M CHOPPIN' EVERY SINGLE MORNIN'
AND EVERY SINGLE NIGHT
EVERY HAIR I CLIP I FEEL CONNECTED TO
LIKE THE PERSON I'M AFFECTING WAS DIRECTED TO MY CHAIR
WAS I CUT OUT FOR GREATNESS
WHEN THE DOCTORS CUT MY CORD?
HAVE I BEEN STYLED TO HEAD TO WHERE I'M HEADING
TOWARD?
I SEE THEIR FACES LEAVING
BRIGHT AND SHINING, AND I'M BLESSED
YOU ASK ME ALL THESE QUESTIONS, I SAY
...NEXT

PATRON 1

WHEN I COME TO THE BARBERSHOP
I FEEL MAGIC IN THE AIR
NOTHIN'S QUITE LIKE THE FEEL OF HOT
FOAM ON YOUR FACE AND IN YOUR HAIR

BILL

ESTABLISHED 1922 BY MY OLD
GREAT GRANDPA MCCALE
WE'VE BEEN HERE EVER SINCE BECAUSE
WHEN YOU'RE A BARBER

5

BILL AND JOEL

YOU CAN'T FAIL

Dance break. No prisoners.

PATRONS AND BARBER TRIO

WE'RE ALL RAVING
JOEL, YOU'RE SHAVING
CLOSER THAN THE BEST
BILL'S SUCCESSOR, BEST HAIRDRESSER

BARBER TRIO

OOOH! WE'RE SO IMPRESSED!

PATRONS, BARBER TRIO, AND BILL

OOOH! WE'RE SO IMPRESSED!

PATRONS AND BILL	BARBER TRIO	JOEL
GOOD MORNING MONDAY, MY FAVORITE TIME THE PERFECT START TO A PERFECT WEEK GOOD MORNING JOEL, IT'S YOUR TIME TO SHINE SO PUT THAT RAZOR TO MY CHEEK, OH OH OH WE'RE GONNA HOP HOP HOP TILL OUR TROUBLES MELT AWAY WE'RE GONNA STOP STOP STOP BY THE BARBERSHOP	COME DROP BY THE BARBERSHOP YOU GOTTA HOP HOP HOP TO THE BARBERSHOP YOU BETTER STOP STOP STOP BY THE BARBERSHOP YOU BETTER COME BY OUR WAY COME DROP BY THE BARBERSHOP YOU GOTTA HOP HOP HOP TO THE BARBERSHOP YOU BETTER STOP STOP STOP BY THE BARBERSHOP	ALL THIS CUTTING, ALL THIS SHAVING MAKES ME START TO SWOON LIKE I'M IN A DAYDREAM EVERY SINGLE AFTERNOON I CREATE A PERFECT PLACE FOR MAKING PEOPLE'S DAY I'M GONNA STOP STOP STOP BY THE BARBERSHOP

JOEL
YOU'D BETTER COME BY OUR WAY

ALL
YOU'D BETTER COME BY OUR WAY
YOU'D BETTER COME BY OUR WAY

EVERY DAY!

> The BARBER TRIO exits through the back door they came
> through and the customers leave, satisfied. TIMMY enters
> from stage right. He is JOEL's age, maybe a bit younger. He
> doesn't walk so much as amble about, and he exudes an
> easygoing aura. On his way into the barber shop he notices a
> beautiful girl quietly strumming a guitar.

TIMMY
Good morning McCale clan!

JOEL
Timmy!

BILL
Mornin' Timothy.

> TIMMY slides inside and shares an elaborate secret
> handshake with JOEL. During the following lines, a customer
> comes in and BILL begins to cut his hair.

TIMMY
How goes the barber-ing?

JOEL
(With a slight grunt.)
Do you have to keep calling it that?

TIMMY
Why? Does it bug you?

JOEL
You know how much I hate it...

TIMMY
And that, my dear Joel, is why I keep saying it.

7

JOEL
Well, if you must know, it goes well at the moment. How goes the unemployment-ing?

TIMMY
Awh, low blow dude.

JOEL
It wouldn't be if you'd just get a job.

TIMMY
(Blatantly changing the subject.)
Speaking of the ladies, I saw guitar girl again!

JOEL
Yeah?! I mean...Oh, that's nice.

JOEL goes back to mixing lather.

TIMMY
Come on, if you don't go talk to her...I will. I mean, seriously, man, the shop has practically taken over your life lately.

JOEL starts when TIMMY says this and mixes a bit too hard, sending lather flying.

BILL
Shouldn't you be looking for a job, Timothy?

TIMMY
Looking diligently, sir!

(Back to JOEL.)
But seriously--

JOEL
(Silently, as if to keep BILL from overhearing.)
I know, I know, but I think Pop's looking to give me some more responsibility and I've got to show him I'm ready... No matter how much I'd like to get into the world...

TIMMY
I gotcha, man, all I'm saying is you've gotta explore a little. The world and yourself. Staying in this shop twenty four seven will kill you.

JOEL
Well, while I appreciate the concern, I belong here. The McCales have been in this barber shop for seventy years!

BILL
Seventy-five, actually!

JOEL
Oh no, pop, not again.

3. BARBER GENEALOGY

BILL
(In a bad Irish accent.)
WE BEGIN OUR TALE BY THE LOFTY CLIFFS OF MOHER
IN GOOD OL' IRELAND, 1882
MY GREAT, GREAT GRANDPOP OLD MAN CASEY MCCALE
GAZIN' 'CROSS THE GREAT BIG OCEAN BLUE
NOW OLD MAN CASEY WONDER'D 'BOUT THE NEW WORLD
WIT A BOUNCIN BABY, JACOB, ON 'IS HIP
HIS FAMILY, STARVED AND DEAD, LEFT 'IM WITH SIX LOAVES OF BREAD
WHICH BOUGHT 'IM PASSAGE ON A NEARBY SHIP
WHEN 'E AND JACOB CAME TO THE SOUTHERN SHORELINE
THE IRISH-HATERS YELLED AT JACOB'S POP
THE SHOUTIN' TOOK ITS TOLL, AND HE CROAKED, THE POOR OLD SOUL AND JACOB HAD TO WORK IN A BARBERSHOP

TIMMY
Wait, this baby worked in a barbershop?

BILL
Well, of course by this time the kid was seventeen. He took up work out of determination to stay in America and fulfill his father's wishes.

TIMMY
(Beat.)
And the accent?

9

JOEL

Just let him finish.

BILL

Thank you, Joel.
NOW IN THIS TOWN WAS A SCUMMY LOWLIFE MOBSTER
A NO-GOOD HUSTLER TYLER "THE KNIFE" MALONE
WHO WAS SQUEEZING JACOB'S BOSS, TAKIN EVERYTHING HE
GOTS
AND NABBIN EVERY PENNY HE COULD OWN
BUT JACOB WASN'T SITTIN BACK
WHEN HE NOTICED HIS BOSS'S EYE WAS BLACK
HE TROTTED ALONG TO OL' TYLER'S SHACK
HE ROLLED UP HIS SLEEVES AND TAPPED KNIFE ON THE BACK
AND SAID "SIR, I EXPECTED MORE FROM YOU.
NOW PLEASE FORGIVE ME FOR THIS PAIN I INTEND TO INFLICT."

TIMMY

...What?

BILL

SO JACOB GAVE THE KNIFE A RIGHT GOOD LICKIN
TOOK HIS GOLD TEETH AND HIS HOTTY TODDY GIRL
WON HIS MONEY AND HIS STRANGE IN AN OLD IRISH EXCHANGE
AND HERE IS WHERE OUR FAMOUS TALE UNFURLED
YOU PROBABLY WONDER "WHAT ABOUT THE GOLD TEETH?"
WELL, HE FASHIONED THEM INTO A PAIR OF SHEARS
CUT THE RIBBON ON THE FRONT IN A BOLD AND PUBLIC STUNT
THAT GAVE THE MCCALE'S WORK FOR ALL THESE YEARS

BILL (CONT'D)
(JOEL mouths with him.)

1922. Good year.

JOEL

The ending's my favorite part! Why don't you skip to there?

BILL

Absolutely not.
YOUR GREAT GRANDPOP, JOEL, HIS NAME WAS JACKSON
A HANDSOME MAN--HIS WIFE, KAREN, GORGEOUS TOO
BUT NO SON CAME TO KAREN, AND THEY FEARED THAT SHE WAS
BARREN
AND NO ONE COULD COME UP WITH WHAT TO DO
JACKSON STILL HELD TIGHT HIS GOLDEN SCISSORS
AND TRIED TO THINK OF WAYS THAT THEY COULD COPE
BUT BEFORE HE HAD TO TRY THIS, CAME THE CUBAN MISSILE
CRISIS
AND BABY JAKE SHOT OUT LIKE A BAR OF SOAP

TIMMY

Whoa dude. Whoa.

JOEL

End please.

BILL

Almost there, boys.
JAKE WAS NAMED FOR HIS OLD SCRAPPY GRANDPOP
MY OLD POP TAUGHT ME EVERYTHING I KNOW
LIKE OUR PERFECT FAMILY TREE, AND OUR FAMILY HISTORY

(Pick up the tempo.)
AND HE GAVE ME THIS BEFORE HE DIED AND NOW MY SON
YOU'RE BONA FIDE THE READIEST YOU'LL EVER BE SO HERE MY
SON YES HERE YOU GO.

BILL gives him the scissors. After this scene, the scissors
should hang on the wall in the barbershop in plain sight.

JOEL

The family shears! You're sure pop?

BILL

More sure than I've ever been of anything. These are yours, Joel. I'm
so proud of you son.

JOEL and BILL share a moment and embrace.

BILL (CONT'D)

Well, I'm going to head on home I think, I trust you can close 'er up?

JOEL

Sure thing pop.

      Bill grabs his coat and goes to leave the shop, but stops on his way out the door.

BILL

Love you kid.

JOEL

You too pop.

      Exit BILL.

ACT ONE, SCENE 3

JOEL
And that, my dear Timmy, is why I've spent so much time here.

TIMMY
Congrats man, but that's a little bit more than a little bit more responsibility.

JOEL
Yeah, that was a little bit more than I was expecting. But hey, not gonna complain about the plan being a little ahead of schedule.

TIMMY
Your plan? I mean, I get that this is what you've been groomed for this whole time, but can you really say it's your plan?

JOEL
Well it's been my life up until now...cutting hair is what I know, and it makes me happy. What would I do if not this?

TIMMY
Don't you have other dreams? What happened to that time you wanted to be the next Michelle Kwon?

JOEL
(A little scared.)
That was just a phase.

(Beat.)
And sure, I've had other dreams, but this is the most practical. It makes sense. I am a McCale after all. I can't just go be any old nonsense.

TIMMY
I hear you loud and clear. I'm happy for you so long as you're sure about this.

JOEL
I'm sure. And it's not like I can't go exploring life. Pop's not handing over the shop to me completely.

TIMMY

Nah, man.

(Gesturing to the shop.)
This is your life now.

JOEL

Why do you gotta be such a bummer, man? Just be happy for me.

TIMMY

I am! Honest, I am. It's just that I want you to be sure.
Isn't there anything else you like more than being a barber?

JOEL

(Beat.)
Making other people happy.

TIMMY

Of course.

JOEL

No, really!

4. BARBERSHOP TALES (REPRISE 1)

JOEL (CONT'D)
THE ONLY THING I CARE ABOUT IS MAKING PEOPLE SMILE

TIMMY
WHY NOT THINK ABOUT YOURSELF A LITTLE WHILE?

JOEL
CUSTOMER SATISFACTION IS THE ONLY THING I NEED

TIMMY
WAIT, HOW LONG HAVE WE BEEN SINGING?

JOEL
Just for a few bars.

TIMMY
Oh, that's not too bad. Anyway man, congrats again. What are you
gonna do with those fancy shears, by the way?

14

JOEL

Oh these babies are going on the wall right next to the McCale lineage chart!

TIMMY

Yeah, speaking of... Color me skeptical but something makes me seriously doubt the factual integrity of ol' Bill's story.
I mean I can believe...

(Ad lib till cut off by JOEL.)

JOEL

Shh! Do you hear that?

> An acoustic guitar rendition of "I Love You" has been wafting
> through the air for a bit. Its source is the beautiful girl sitting
> on the bench across the street, with a dilapidated guitar.

TIMMY

Hear what?

JOEL

It's her.

TIMMY

Oh! Guitar girl!

JOEL

Would that she were mine, I would take her in sweet embrace and whisper sweet nothings till dawn's break, as her sweet mellifluous melodies meander through the misty mountain meadows 'neath the mellow moonlight!

> JOEL swoons and sighs.

TIMMY

Dude.

JOEL

Dude?

TIMMY

DUDE. Go! Talk! To! Her!

JOEL

Can't I watch her from here?

TIMMY

That's extremely creepy and no! Go over there and put the moves on her!

JOEL
(Getting more frazzled.)
I don't even know what that means!

TIMMY

Follow your heart kemosabe!

JOEL

What?!

TIMMY

TALK TO HER.

JOEL

I CAN'T!

TIMMY

YOU CAN!

JOEL

I CAN'T!

5. JUST CAN'T STAY AWAY

TIMMY

IF YOU'RE LOOKIN' AT HER YOU AT LEAST SHOULD SAY HELLO

JOEL

YOU CAN'T TRY TO UNDERSTAND IT

TIMMY

HOW WILL YOU GET ANYWHERE WHEN YOU MOVE SO DAMN SLOW?

JOEL

IT'S NOT LIKE I
COULD HAVE PLANNED IT
YOU JUST HAVE TO WALK A DAY IN MY SHOES

BARBER TRIO

WALKIN ON BY

JOEL

JUST TO SEE THAT
I'M NOT PLAYIN'
I'M WAITIN'-

TIMMY

TELL ME WHAT YOU HAVE TO LOSE?

TIMMY (CONT'D)

You got nothin'!

JOEL

STILL, I'M STAYIN'.
I CAN'T GET HER OFF MY MIND WHENEVER-

TIMMY

DUDE, YOU NEED TO TALK OR SHUT UP

JOEL

ISN'T SHE SO PERFECT IN THIS WEATHER?

TIMMY

KEEP IT TO YOURSELF OR NUT UP
JOEL, YOU HAVE TO UNDERSTAND WHAT NORMAL MEANS
THERE'S A SET OF BASIC GUIDELINES
NORMAL PEOPLE JUST DON'T-

JOEL

(Interrupting.)
JUST LIKE IN MY WILDEST DREAMS
HITS ME LIKE A RAY OF SUNSHINE
SHE WILL BE MINE

TIMMY

YOU SHOULD SEE A DOCTOR, YOU'RE NOT TALKIN' SENSE RIGHT
NOW.

JOEL

I JUST WONDER WHAT HER NAME IS.

TIMMY

TAKE IT FAST OR MAKE IT LAST, JUST MAKE IT START SOMEHOW.
DOESN'T EVEN MATTER WHAT YOUR GAME IS.

JOEL

I JUST WANT TO WAIT.

TIMMY

WALK UP TO HER
OR ACT LIKE YOU NEVER KNEW HER

JOEL

I CAN'T LIVE WITHOUT HER,
CAUSE I JUST CAN'T STAY AWAY

A dance break of sorts.

TIMMY (CONT'D)

Is any of this getting through to you?

JOEL

What? Oh... about fifty percent.

TIMMY

C'mon! I'm getting all soulful here man! At least give me some credit!

JOEL

I CAN HEAR THE ANGELS EVERY TIME SHE PLAYS DOESN'T MEAN
THAT I AM CRAZY

TIMMY

I'M NOT SAYIN' YOU SHOULD CHANGE YOUR WAYS YOU JUST
SHOULDN'T BE SO LAZY

JOEL

GIVE ME ONE MORE DAY

JUDY

Hi, I'm Judy.

> Super awkward pause.
> TIMMY pats JOEL on the back. Exit TIMMY.

JOEL

...uh...hi?

JUDY
(Sizing him up.)
You're that singing barber kid right?

JOEL

Oh yeah, I'm Joel.

> JOEL extends his hand.

JUDY

Pleased to meet you Joel!

> JUDY shakes his hand.

JOEL
Uh... I heard you playing guitar earlier!

JUDY
Oh yeah! I play out here a lot actually, I'm surprised we haven't run into each other before.

JOEL
Well you know, I keep pretty busy with the shop.

JUDY
You run that big old place by yourself?

JOEL
Well my dad owns and operates it, but I work there and he gives me a cut of the profits.

On the word "cut", JOEL cuts an imaginary head of hair with the shears. Barber humor...
Judy smiles at his barber humor. Joel suddenly fumbles the shears and they tumble toward the ground. Judy deftly snatches them with cat-like reflexes.

JOEL (CONT'D)

Hey! Nice shave.

More barber humor. PLAY IT UP.
JOEL and JUDY both burst into laughter, both snorting loudly at the same time. The connection between them clicks immediately as they both realize their shared snorting.

JOEL AND JUDY

Whoa!

They both laugh again at their simultaneous exclamations and grin at one another.

JUDY

Do you like...

JOEL
(Finishing her sentence.)

Pineapples?

JOEL AND JUDY

Yes!

More laughing. More snorting. Absolutely adorable.

JUDY

This is too weird.

JOEL

You're telling me! Stuff like this never happens to me.

JUDY

Me neither.

Both are practically beaming at this point.

JUDY (CONT'D)

Would you like to take a walk with me? I mean I'm not some kind of creeper or anything but, you just seem cool and... Yeah.

JOEL

I would! But... I sorta have to be heading home right now.

JUDY

Oh! That's fine. No problem.

JOEL

But... rain check?

JUDY
(Presenting the shears to him.)
I would be honored, sir!

JOEL

Awesome.

JUDY
(Smiling.)
See you later... Joel.

JUDY hefts her guitar and exits. JOEL is left dumbfounded.

5a. JUST CAN'T STAY AWAY (REPRISE)

JOEL

I'M SIX THOUSAND MILES HIGH WHEN SHE IS HERE
NO ONE COULD RESIST THAT BEAUTY I'VE
NEVER KNOWN OF ANYTHING SO CLEAR
I THINK I'M IN LOVE WITH JUDY
IT MAY BE TOO FAST BUT I'M PRAYING
HARDLY KNOW HER? STILL I'M STAYING
MAKES ME FEEL ALL SNUGGLY
NOW I JUST CAN'T STAY AWAY

Exit JOEL. Blackout.

ACT ONE, SCENE 4

Lights up on the town. BILL is in the barber shop, during the following action he goes about normal shop business. BUBBA stands outside the barber shop, smoking a cigarette. On the bench nearby, three homeless people sit; ALEX, CAROL, and DAVID. They are dressed in raggedy patchwork clothing. ALEX, sitting between the other two, whittles away at a small piece of wood with a jackknife.

DAVID
What you got there Alex? Piece of driftwood?

ALEX
Tree branch actually. I've decided to start whittling and sell what I make down on fifth.

DAVID
Whittling, eh? And that there's your first piece of work?

ALEX holds up a mutilated piece of wood.

ALEX
Yeah. It's coming along quite nicely. I think the starving artist career fits me quite nicely, don't it?

CAROL
Seems to me that you're already halfway there. Good luck with your modern art, I for one prefer to make my way with a more traditional panhandling tactic.

CAROL pulls out a flat piece of cardboard with a scrawled message on it along the lines of "Need $$$ for eye operation." ALEX and DAVID let out a groan.

ALEX
Great. The sign.

DAVID
Classic Carol.

CAROL
(Somewhat bewildered.)
What do you mean? You don't like the sign? This sign is a gold mine!

ALEX
It most certainly is not a gold mine, it's an old, moldy piece of cardboard. You're not gonna get squat from anyone with that nasty old thing.

CAROL
Oh yeah, sure. Like your little totem pole is gonna get you more than two cents and a few fingers full of splinters. This sign is classic.

DAVID
Sure, it may be classic but I for one feel like you're way overdue for a new piece of cardboard there.

CAROL
Well if you've got one, Dave, I would be glad to relieve you of it.

DAVID
Nah, I don't carry cardboard around. It's all plastics nowadays. Don't believe in signs as an effective form of conveyance anyway.

ALEX
You don't? Why?

DAVID
I'm personally part of the school of thought that believes auditory stimuli trumps visual every time.

CAROL
What draws you to that particular theory?

DAVID
Well, the way I see it, written language is a construct that has come about as a result of thousands of years of spoken language. Logically, early humans communicated verbally long before written language was even beginning to arise. This leads me to believe that our minds are much more comfortable with processing language in terms of auditory information as opposed to visual.

CAROL

I see where you're coming from, but you're forgetting that body language is a huge, albeit subconscious, part of communication. Nonverbal communication seems to lend itself much more to the visual than the auditory. So if you ask me to choose between a phonetic cue and a written one I would-

> TIMMY enters stage right. ALEX notices him immediately.

ALEX

Oh, we got an ambler.

DAVID

Dibs.

CAROL

Dibs. Awh crap. Snooze you lose!

> ALEX, DAVID, and CAROL leap up and run over to TIMMY, pushing and shoving amongst themselves to solicit him for money

ALEX	CAROL	DAVID	ALEX
Hey man, can you spare me a buck?	I'm real sick, I just need some cash for medicine.	Have a heart man, I'm a veteran, I got a kid man!	I just need some cash for gas, then I'm gone man. You see I've got a family up in Montana-

> CAROL coughs violently, like she is dying. BILL notices the hullabaloo and moves to exit the shop.

TIMMY

I uh... I've only got my debit card on me?

> The homeless trio erupts into a new cacophony of ad-libbed complaints and pleadings. BILL swings the door open, holding a broom.

BILL

You lot clear out of here! I said clear out!

CAROL
(Quietly to DAVID and ALEX.)
Awh, great. The old stiff who runs the barber shop.

BILL
I catch you panhandling around here again and I'm calling the cops.

The three exchange nervous glances.

BILL (CONT'D)
I mean it! Now go on! Go shake someone else down.

The homeless trio scatters and exits. TIMMY sighs, relieved.

TIMMY
Thanks, Bill. I think you gave the short one a heart attack.

BILL
(Sternly.)
If they're not going to bother working, they might as well have the decency to not bother the ones who've gotta work for a living...

(Now pleasantly.)
So, Timothy m'boy, what can I do for you?

TIMMY
Is Joel in?

BILL
Sure is, come on in.

They enter the barbershop.

ACT ONE, SCENE 5

As soon as TIMMY enters the shop, a BARBERSHOP RAG begins playing. ELLIE and RACHEL are cutting the hair of two patrons. They're the last customers of the day. JOEL is taking his apron off as BILL and TIMMY enter.

BILL
(Ad lib until he sees JOEL.)
Where are you running off to? We still gotta close up.

JOEL
Uh, actually I was thinking of taking the evening off, if that's OK.

BILL hands TIMMY a broom, and hangs his apron upon him. Could you hold these for me real quick?

TIMMY
Uh...

BILL
That's fine. I just wish you had told me earlier so we could have rescheduled Pizza Night. You got a hot date or something?

JOEL
(Sheepishly.)
Actually...

BILL
(Surprised.)
Oh! Well good on you kid. Gonna be out late?

JOEL
I'm not sure, I'll text you sometime tonight.

BILL
Ok, well don't forget your coat, there's a cold front coming in.

JOEL
Sure thing, pop.

JOEL notices TIMMY awkwardly standing with the broom.

TIMMY

So should I-

JOEL

Sorry man, I can't really hang out right now.

TIMMY

Oh, no dude, it's cool. Don't wait up man.

JOEL

Thanks dude, see you. Bye Pop!

> JOEL runs out the door as the customers pay BILL at the
> counter. After they leave, he turns the sign over to CLOSED
> and flicks the lit-up barber pole off, he then goes to sweep up.

TIMMY

So... is Charlie in today?

ELLIE

Does it look like she's in?

TIMMY

Oh, I... thought she might be in the back or something...

RACHEL

The back? Why would she possibly be in the back?

TIMMY

I don't know! Maybe she'd be getting shaving cream...

> ELLIE and RACHEL stare him down.

TIMMY (CONT'D)

...or something.

ELLIE

Well she's not here... so leave.

RACHEL

Yeah!

TIMMY backs away warily, looking thoroughly frightened. The girls continue to stare him down. BILL watches the exchange, his hands frozen mid-sweep. Finally the ice breaks and the girls begin to giggle.

ELLIE
Ohmigawd, we're totally messing with you.

RACHEL
Ohmigawd. For real.

TIMMY
Oh man, you guys had me going.

ELLIE
Yeah, we did.

ELLIE and RACHEL high five, then return to cleaning the shop, ignoring TIMMY. This continues for a few beats.

TIMMY
So uh... did she go home or is she coming back?

ELLIE
What do you need her for?

RACHEL
Yeah, what do you even neeeed her for?

ELLIE
What are you, her manager, or something?

TIMMY
Actually that's Bill.

RACHEL
(Running over TIMMY'S previous line.)
What are you, her mom?

ELLIE
What are you, watering her plants?

RACHEL

What are you, her fashion consultant?

ELLIE

Writing her biography?

RACHEL

Picking up her groceries?

ELLIE

Cleaning her pool?

RACHEL

Returning her videos?

TIMMY

What?!

ELLIE

(Sneering.)
What are you, taking her on a date?

RACHEL

Yeah! Are you taking her on a date?

ELLIE

You don't have any flowers. Charlie only dates guys who bring flowers.

RACHEL

Yeah, no flowers, no date.

ELLIE

Where's the chocolates?

RACHEL

Yeah! The chocolates. Where are they?

ELLIE

You should know these things Timmy. How are you gonna get Charlie if you don't know these things?

Meanwhile, TIMMY ad libs, flounders horribly in response.

BILL

Ah, dating. I remember dating. The old days, biking down to the corner soda shop. Summer love... so fleeting. It was hotter back then you know, and I'm not just talking about the weather if you catch my drift.

> (Everyone is uncomfortable. BILL brings TIMMY in close.)

Son, if you ever need any tips about women. You know, I used to be quite the ladies' man.

TIMMY

I'M NOT GOING ON A DATE WITH CHARLIE!

> Silence for a moment. Then CHARLIE enters from the back room, carrying a large box. Everyone is staring at her, it's blaringly apparent that she has heard what TIMMY shouted.

CHARLIE

Hey Timmy.

TIMMY

> (Nervously.)

‚Hey Charlie.

> (Beat.)

Whatcha got there?

CHARLIE

Just some shaving cream.

TIMMY

Of course it is... I'll just show myself out.

> TIMMY exits out the front door, continuing off stage left. Charlie begins setting the cans of shaving cream at each barber-station, putting the excess cans beneath the front desk. BILL grabs his coat and hat.

BILL

You girls can close up, right?

30

CHARLIE

Sure thing Mr. McCale.

ELLIE

Yeah, no problem.

BILL

Great. See you tomorrow.

BILL exits. For a moment, the shop is quiet, but soon the sounds of cleaning and closing fill the room as the girls go to work picking up the shop. CHARLIE quietly goes about her work showing no emotion.

ELLIE

So Rachel, how did your date with Danny last night go?

RACHEL

It was nice. We caught the double feature at the theater in Bloomsdale.

ELLIE

Ooooh, how romantic! Playing tonsil hockey in the back row eh?

RACHEL

Ew, Ellie cut it out!

CHARLIE
(Finally breaking her silence).

I'm not hearing a no!

RACHEL turns bright red while ELLIE and CHARLIE giggle at her embarrassment.

ELLIE

At least she's learning right?

RACHEL

I mean Danny's OK, but he's kind of a slob. I don't think I see us panning out in the long run.

CHARLIE

Oh, heart breaker! You better watch out, guys dig heartbreakers.

RACHEL rolls her eyes good naturedly.

CHARLIE (CONT'D)
I'm serious! You better watch out. All the boys are going to be flocking to you in droves once they find out you're a devil in disguise.

RACHEL
Just like you, huh Charlie?

CHARLIE
Well, I think we've just seen that's not really the case.

Beat.

ELLIE
What, you mean Timmy? We were just messing around with him, and then he just freaked out.

RACHEL
Yeah, he was totally overreacting.

ELLIE
Totally.

CHARLIE is quiet once again, not paying attention.

ELLIE (CONT'D)
Wait, you don't...

CHARLIE
What?

ELLIE
Never mind.

The girls grab their coats and move towards the door as CHARLIE goes to turn the lights out. The stage darkens completely except for the barber pole, which flickers for a moment in the darkness, then goes out.

ACT ONE, SCENE 6

> The lights are off in the barbershop, only a streetlight near the bench provides illumination. JUDY sits upon the bench, sewing something. JOEL enters from stage right, hair combed and sporting a tie. He walks toward JUDY.

JOEL

Hey.

> JUDY hurriedly puts the sewing equipment aside.

JUDY

Joel! Hey!

JOEL

Sorry I'm late.

> (Gesturing at his tie.)

I couldn't figure out how to tie this stupid thing.

JUDY

Don't worry about it. I was just out here enjoying the evening.

JOEL

It is quite lovely out.

> He sits down next to her.

JOEL (CONT'D)

> (Looking up.)

The stars are gorgeous tonight...

JUDY

Just like always...

JOEL

What are you making?

JUDY

Hmm?

> JOEL points at her sewing paraphernalia.

JUDY (CONT'D)
Oh! I was just patching up an old dress of mine.

JOEL
That's really cool! Do you fix a lot of clothes?

JUDY
Now that I think about it, yeah. I guess I'm sort of the tailor for my group of friends. It's really nice to be able to help out people, you know?

JOEL
How long have you been sewing for?

JUDY
Well, longer than I can remember. I've always loved clothing. When I was a kid, I used to walk all the way downtown just so I could see the beautiful dresses that were on display in the shop windows. I could never afford them though, so I learned how to sew. That way, I'd be able to preserve what mom and I had. Since then I've always just sort of been sewing for anyone who needs it. But I guess the real reason I fix things is because it's what Mom always did.

JOEL
She sounds like an amazing woman.

JUDY
Yeah, she really was...

6. THE MOST WONDERFUL CAREER

JUDY (CONT'D)
OLD, DIRTY RAGS
AND RIPPED PANTYHOSE
A GIRL CAN'T FORGET THESE
WHENEVER SHE SEWS
BEAUTIFUL PEOPLE WHEREVER SHE GOES
LOOK AT THEM SULKING
IN TORN, TATTERED CLOTHES
I DARE TO CARE
TO WANT MORE FOR THEM

FABULOUS SHE-VAGRANT 1
(Raspily, of course.)
How do I look, Judy?

JUDY
Marvelous, Janet, simply divine.

(Upbeat softshoe.)

MOM SAID
COUNT ON YOUR DAYDREAMS
FOLLOW YOUR HEART THEY'LL COME TRUE
WHEN I
GIVE 'EM SOME FASHION
I KNOW THEY NEVER COME OUT BLUE
IT STARTED WITH A DASH OF INSPIRATION
JUST LIKE THE GREATEST ENTERPRISES DO
NOW EVERY DAY I SPIN AWAY THEIR THREADS INTO GOLD
AND GIVE THEM A BRAND NEW DEBUT
I LOVE
THESE SMILES IN THE MAKING
TRIMMING THE SADNESS OFF OF EACH FACE
HIGH FASHION
NO REASON THIS BURLAP
CAN'T BE AS FINE AS SATIN, VELVET, OR LACE

FABULOUS SHE-VAGRANT 2
IT'S LIKE I'M WINNING PROM QUEEN
I'M SNOW WHITE AT THE BALL

FABULOUS SHE-VAGRANT 3
THIS EVENING GOWN MAKES ME FEEL LIKE A PORCELAIN DOLL

JUDY
IT'S GENUINELY FEMININE
THESE GIRLS HAVE IT ALL WHEN I PATCH A NEW BATCH OF
GOWNS!

FABULOUS SHE-VAGRANTS
WE LOVE
THE AD HOC ENSEMBLES
AND OUR DESIGNER GENIUS TOO

35

JUDY

WHO?

FABULOUS SHE-VAGRANTS

YOU!

FABULOUS SHE-VAGRANT 1

(In a particularly unflattering and raspy New York
accent.)

Of course.

FABULOUS SHE-VAGRANTS

TURNING
OUR RAGS INTO RICHES

JUDY

FOLLOW YOUR HEART, IT COMES TRUE

FABULOUS SHE-VAGRANT 1

Softshoe!

A very tasteful softshoe dance break.

FABULOUS SHE-VAGRANTS & JUDY

Yeah!

JOEL

Judy that's fantastic!

JUDY

Awh, it's not that impressive.

JOEL

It really is though. You're extremely talented, and I think that what
you're doing with your talent is really awesome.

JUDY

Thanks Joel. It's just, sometimes I wish that I could do more...

JOEL

Hey, you do enough already. Look how happy you've made these
people. You're helping the world, one person at a time. And I think
that's great.

JUDY

(Genuinely.)

Thanks.

JOEL

Now how about we take that walk I promised you?

JUDY

That sounds just lovely.

They link arms and walk. Lights down.

ACT ONE, SCENE 7

Lights come back up on the barbershop. Inside the shop is
MAC, a middle aged man who sits patiently reading a
magazine. ALEX snores loudly outside on the bench, while
CAROL and DAVID walk on bickering. Suddenly CAROL,
taking notices, shushes DAVID.

CAROL

BOO!

ALEX

WHAT IN-- You... you sack of potatoes, David! Why, I've got half a
mind to

(Ad lib.)

CAROL

(Interrupting.)
That's right, old man, you sure do have half a mind. What'd you do
with the rest, anyway? The pigeons take it for bread or something?

DAVID

Hush up you two, I think I found something!

(Pulls a tattered jacket from behind the tree.)
This is a vintage! People just don't know fashion anymore.

DAVID slides into the jacket, revealing a large hole in the
back.

CAROL

Yeah, you get something excellent like that and they look right
through it.

ALEX

Say, yeah, that's pretty slick. Looks like you got the 'hole' package...

CAROL

So...aerodynamic!

DAVID continues to admire his jacket, completely oblivious.

38

ALEX

There's a giant tear in the back of your jacket.

DAVID

Awh snickers!

ALEX

No, it's alright. I actually know a girl who fixes up this sort of thing.

CAROL

A tailor? How long have you been bourgeois, Alex?

DAVID

In what capacity does a tailor indicate class? Everyone needs a good tailor.

ALEX

Everyone needs a good tailor, everyone needs a good barber. Speaking of which, WE GOT AN AMBLER!

They heckle a CUSTOMER leaving the barbershop, who frantically tries to avoid them without causing a scene. They follow the CUSTOMER offstage. Meanwhile, lights focus on the barbershop, and JOEL comes out of the back room, whistling jovially. He sees MAC and greets him heartily.

JOEL

Morning Mac!

MAC

My man Joel!

JOEL

You here for the usual?

MAC

Sure, sure... Actually, mix it up a little today.

JOEL

That I can do sir.

He seats MAC in the barber chair and goes about cutting his hair.

39

JOEL (CONT'D)

How are you doing this fine day sir?

MAC

Been worse my boy. Yourself?

JOEL

I feel fantastic sir.

MAC

That so?

JOEL

Indeed! Things have just been going my way lately.

MAC

My innate senses tell me that a lovely lady may have a hand in this, am I right?

JOEL

You are.

MAC

Nothin' can quite bring a smile to a man's face like the affections of a beautiful girl, ah?

JOEL

She's... so real, you know? We met a few weeks ago and instantly hit it off. She's smart and kind, she laughs at all my jokes...

MAC

Always a good sign.

JOEL

Yeah! She's always making things out of old stuff too. I mean, last night when we were walking she pulled an old umbrella out of a trash can and all she could talk about was how she could turn it into a dress.

MAC

Oh wow, so she's the artsy type?

JOEL

Definitely, she has a great eye for fixing up old things and making them into something new. She's also a musician!

MAC

That so? You go to any of her gigs?

JOEL

Oh, she doesn't play for money really. I mean people sometimes drop a little cash into her case but she does it because she just loves to play.

MAC

I think I may know this girl, is she...

He describes JUDY physically.

JOEL

Yeah, that sounds just like Judy! She plays guitar outside the shop sometimes.

MAC

Yeah, yeah! I know her.

JOEL

I figured that you had seen her.

MAC

She is quite pretty indeed. You're a lucky man!

JOEL

Thank you kindly sir.

MAC

I always thought that she was homeless.

Classic sloppy drum drop, as if the entire pit simultaneously fell over. JOEL is taken completely off guard by the statement and the electric razor in his hand slips, shaving a crooked half of a mohawk into the elderly man's hair.

JOEL
(In regards to both happenings.)
Oh crap.

MAC
What? What's going on back there?

MAC grabs the nearest mirror.

MAC (CONT'D)
Oh my God... I love it.

JOEL
(Completely shocked.)
It's on the house Mac.

MAC
Awh thanks, pal. Good luck with your lady!

MAC exits the shop as CHARLIE enters she does a double take as MAC walks by.

CHARLIE
Joel, did you just cut Mac's hair?

JOEL
Yeah. I've never slipped up that badly before. He loved it.

CHARLIE
(Staring after MAC.)
Mac's a little strange...

JOEL
He said he thought that Judy was homeless.

CHARLIE
What? That's ridiculous.

JOEL
Yeah, I know but as weird as it sounds it sort of makes sense.

CHARLIE
What do you mean?

JOEL

Just little things that she says and does.

CHARLIE

I do see her out by that bus stop a lot.

JOEL

(Exasperated.)
Great, the girl of my dreams might actually be a hobo.

CHARLIE

Don't freak out Joel. Try to think back to when you met her.

JOEL

OK, OK. Um... Pop had just given me the family shears... and Timmy
and I were outside the shop talking...

> As he describes what is happening, the lights change and
> JOEL moves toward the spot where he and TIMMY were
> talking before and during "Just Can't Stay Away." TIMMY and
> JUDY enter from stage right and crosses to the spots they
> were in as well.
> The flashback is a sort of set up, like we're getting a glimpse
> into JOEL'S memory, except CHARLIE is there as well.

JOEL (CONT'D)

We were talking about Judy I think... and I said:

> (Rushing through, muttering in tune but not
> necessarily in time.)

I CAN HEAR THE ANGELS EVERY TIME SHE PLAYS
DOESN'T MEAN THAT I AM CRAZY

JOEL (CONT'D)

Then Timmy said:

TIMMY

(Also muttering.)
I'M NOT SAYIN' YOU SHOULD CHANGE YOUR WAYS
YOU JUST SHOULDN'T BE SO LAZY

JOEL

Then I said:
GIVE ME ONE MORE DAY

JUDY
(Interrupting.)
HI I'M HOMELESS!

JOEL

Oh God, she's totally homeless.

> The lights come back up and they all move back to where
> they were.

CHARLIE

Oh come on Joel, you can't just jump to conclusions like that. Do you
know any of her friends?

JOEL

No...I've only seen her with the people she fixes clothing for.

CHARLIE

Well then the only way you're going to figure it out is by asking her...
tactfully.

> At this moment, TIMMY busts into the shop for real this time.
> He holds aloft a pair of safety scissors in his hand. CHARLIE
> smiles as he enters

TIMMY
(Singing.)
THESE ARE MY FRIENDS.

JOEL

Not now man!

TIMMY

But you love that show.

JOEL

Yeah, but that doesn't change the fact that Judy may be homeless!

TIMMY

Whoa, whoa, whoa, what?

CHARLIE

He doesn't know that for sure.

TIMMY

I guess I did see her digging through a dumpster once or twice before...

JOEL

WHAT?!

TIMMY

Kidding! You're really fired up about this, huh?

JOEL

Of course I am! It's kind of a big deal.

TIMMY

Well you know what you have to do right?

JOEL

Ignore the problem till it goes away?

TIMMY

You've gotta ask her dude.

CHARLIE

Thank you Timmy! That's exactly what I said!

TIMMY

Well uh, you know, great minds think alike.

JOEL

I gotta clear my head, can you handle the shop today Charlie?

CHARLIE

Of course, your dad will be in soon I'm sure.

JOEL

Thanks. I'll see you guys...

JOEL puts up his apron then wanders out of the shop and exits right. CHARLIE grabs a broom and starts sweeping some of the hair from MAC'S haircut.

CHARLIE
That boy gets so uptight about things sometimes.

TIMMY
(Snipping with the scissors then chuckling.)
Hey, cut the kid some slack.

CHARLIE
(Giggling.)
That one never gets old. Where did you get those anyway?

TIMMY
Oh, I had these from high school.

CHARLIE
You used safety scissors in high school?

TIMMY
(Embarrassed.)
Well, I almost snipped my pinky off with regular ones so my teachers made me use these.

CHARLIE
Wow... you know you could have just lied and told me they were your little brother's.

TIMMY
Ah! Hindsight is 20/20 right? I've never even told Joel that story.

CHARLIE
Don't worry. Your safety scissor secret is safe with me.

TIMMY
Nice alliteration!

CHARLIE
I thought it was pretty good, thank you for noticing.

They smile at each other. TIMMY starts to look extremely nervous.

TIMMY
So, hey... I wanted to ask you something...

CHARLIE
Yeah? Go for it.

TIMMY pauses for a moment. The tension becomes almost unbearable, then comes crashing down.

TIMMY
But I just totally forgot what it was.

BILL enters from stage left.

CHARLIE
Awh man, I hate it when that happens!

TIMMY
I know, it's the worst right?

BILL walks into the shop.

BILL
Morning Charlie, Morning Timothy.

CHARLIE
Hey Mr. McCale.

TIMMY
Howdy sir!

BILL looks around the room.

BILL
Is Joel in the back room?

TIMMY and CHARLIE share a look.

CHARLIE
No, he took the day off. I don't think he was feeling too well.

TIMMY

Yeah, he said that he'd be back later.

BILL

Oh, he didn't tell me he was feeling sick. I hope that he's alright.

TIMMY

Oh, he didn't look bad, just needed some fresh air I think.

BILL

OK. Are you going to see him later Tim?

TIMMY

Most likely, yes.

BILL

Well if you see him, just let him know that I'm gonna be at the shop late and I'd like him to swing by to talk for a bit.

TIMMY

Will do sir.

Blackout.

ACT ONE, SCENE 8

> It's the evening. JOEL wanders the streets in search of JUDY. He carries a sizeable box under his arm. He looks like he's been searching for some time now. Homeless people dot the stage, wandering aimlessly.

JOEL

Judy! JUDY!

> A trash can falls over behind him, he whirls about at the sound.

JOEL (CONT'D)

Judy?

> A HOMELESS PERSON stumbles out from the garbage and toward JOEL.

HOMELESS MAN

Maahh namesh not Choody.

JOEL

Oh my...

HOMELESS MAN

Have you sssheen maaah ssshooosh?

JOEL

I have to go... sorry...

> JOEL runs away from the HOBO, running smack dab into TIMMY, who was wandering around stage between homeless people, searching for JOEL.

JOEL (CONT'D)

Timmy? What are you doing out here?!

TIMMY

Looking for you man! You've been gone for hours, dude. Your dad is worried about you.

JOEL

He is? Jeez...

TIMMY

Yeah, he's been waiting practically all night at the shop for you. Said he wanted to talk to you when you got back.

JOEL
(Sighing.)
I have a pretty good idea about what he may want to talk about.

JOEL sits down on the curb, TIMMY follows suit.

TIMMY

Yeah?

JOEL

Yeah. It's the shop. I just...my heart hasn't been in it, lately. I've been thinking a lot about what you said earlier, Timmy. Taking over the shop isn't my plan.

TIMMY

Have you ever talked with your dad about?

JOEL

No way, man. That would crush him. I mean, he's had this plan laid out for me my whole life. But between what you said...and how sure Judy is of what she wants, and what makes her happy. If I'm honest with myself...I've never felt that working in the shop, you know?

TIMMY

I know. We grew up together, man. I get it. As long as I've known you, I've felt like you're meant for more. I can't tell you how to live your life, but I can say that talking with your dad can't hurt.

JOEL

I'll think about it man. I've got a lot on my mind right now though, and I really need to find Judy.

JUDY walks out of a nearby group of homeless people towards where JOEL and TIMMY sit.

TIMMY

Speaking of Judy...

JUDY

Joel?

> Awkward silence ensues. TIMMY does the same awkward pat that he used at the end of 'Just can't stay away' then exits.

JUDY (CONT'D)

What are you doing out here?

JOEL

I had the same question for you...

> JUDY looks at JOEL, kind of off put, as though she has just been sarcastically insulted.

JOEL (CONT'D)
(Solemnly.)

Judy, are you homeless?

JUDY

...Yes.

JOEL

Ok... Ok... That's ok.

JUDY
(A bit defensively.)

That's "OK"?

JOEL

Yes. Yes, it's ok.

JUDY

Are you high?

JOEL

What?!

JUDY

Joel, I'm homeless! Did you not know that?

JOEL
(Remaining calm.)
Well, I guess I overlooked a few details...

JUDY
A few details? Joel, come on, it's not like I've been hiding it from you.

JOEL
Sorry, I just didn't realize.

JUDY
Well now you do. So since you've figured out my big "secret," I guess you'll be leaving, just like everyone else does.

JOEL
Why in the world would you think that?

> JUDY looks at JOEL, confused but enamored. Music begins to play.

JUDY
I guess...I guess I just don't get what you see in me.

7. I LOVE YOU

JOEL

I SEE THE MOON
I SEE THE STARS
I SEE A GIRL
NOT QUITE SO FAR
EVERY NIGHT
EVERY DAY
EVERY LIGHT
SEEMS MILES AWAY

JUDY
Joel, I live on the street. I'm stuck looking at these stupid stars every night. There's nothing under them but a reminder of what I'm not."

JOEL
Exactly.

JUDY

I don't understand.

JOEL

NO, I THINK YOU DO
I'M NOT WITH THE STARS
BUT I'M HERE WITH YOU
AND THE LIGHTS, THE STARS, ALL FLOATING OUT IN SPACE
SEEM TO FADE TO DARKNESS WHEN I SEE YOUR FACE
AND FOR THE LIFE OF ME I CANNOT UNDERSTAND WHY YOU'RE
SO DOWN
I ONLY SEE STARS
WHEN YOU'RE AROUND

                (With tactless confidence, play it up.)
AND I LOVE YOU
EVEN THOUGH YOU ARE HOMELESS
MORE THAN MANY
MAYBE ANY
TREASURES IN THE SKY WHILE YOU'RE WITH ME
YOU CAN NEVER BE HOMELESS
'CAUSE HOME IS EVERYWHERE WHEN YOU'RE THIS HIGH

JOEL (CONT'D)

I got you something.

      JOEL hands her the box. She pulls a pineapple out of the box.

JUDY

You didn't have to give this to me.

JOEL

But Judy, I have so much to give.

JOEL (CONT'D)

I'LL GIVE YOU LOVE
I'LL GIVE YOU STARS
I'LL GIVE YOU HOME
WHEREVER YOU ARE
COME WITH ME, LOVE
JUDY, YOU CAAAN
WE'LL MAKE A HOME
AND I'LL BE YOUR MAN
AND JUDY EVERY SECOND WE'RE APART
IS A SECOND WHEN I'LL NEVER HAVE MORE LONGING IN MY
HEART

JUDY

BUT IF EVERYWHERE IS HOME THEN WHY'S IT SO HARD TO LET
ME GO?

JOEL

YOU'RE NOT JUST MY HOME
I THOUGHT YOU SHOULD KNOW
THAT I LOVE YOU
EVEN THOUGH YOU ARE HOMELESS
NOT TOTALLY
LITERALLY

(Rhyme it.)
BUT YOU GET THE GIST
THAT I LOVE YOU
AND I WON'T LET YOU BE HOMELESS
ALL I ASK FROM YOU
IS ONE SMALL --

The music stops abruptly and cleanly as JUDY passionately
kisses JOEL.
There is a brief musical interlude.

JOEL AND JUDY

AND EVERY SECOND, EVERY MOMENT WE'RE APART
IS A MOMENT THAT I'LL NEVER HAVE MORE LONGING IN MY
HEART

JOEL

AND JUDY, YOU'RE A HOME FOR ME
AND I'M A HOME FOR YOU

JUDY

I HAVE A HOME

JOEL AND JUDY

ALWAYS IN YOU
AND I LOVE YOU
AND WE'LL NEVER BE HOMELESS
ALL THIS LIVING, ALL THIS GIVING
FIN'LLY WE CAN SEE
WHILE OUR LOVE LIVES
WE WILL NEVER BE HOMELESS

JOEL
(Tenderly.)
SO WHY DON'T YOU COME STAY A WHILE
WITH ME

JOEL (CONT'D)
Judy, I know you've been through a lot, and I know there's a lot you want to do. But when I think about this...about us...it just makes me feel so much. So what do you say, Judy? Will you come with me?

JUDY
Joel...I don't know what to say.

JOEL
Yes is a start

JUDY
I...yes!

JOEL
Yes!

JOEL takes a step back.

JUDY
What are you thinking about?

JOEL
(Thinks for a second, playfully and not confused.)
...Cuddling?

JUDY suddenly looks a little dazed.

JOEL (CONT'D)

Oh my gosh, am I moving too fast?

JUDY

No, no! I just didn't even think about everyone I have to say goodbye to.

JOEL

You don't need any goodbyes, Judy. We're not going anywhere. I'm not going anywhere.

    Beat. The two kiss again, passionately.

JOEL (CONT'D)

I don't ever want to stop doing that.

JUDY

Sorry to disappoint, but I just got some breaking news I think I should tell me friends about.

JOEL
       (Playfully.)

Oh yeah? What's that?

JUDY

Oh, you know, nothing important.

JOEL

Well I'll see you tomorrow?

JUDY

I wish, but I promised the girls I'd do some mending work tomorrow. What about Monday?

JOEL
       (Playfully whiny.)

That's so far away...

JUDY

It's only, what, 42 hours?

       She kisses JOEL on the cheek.

I'll be counting the seconds!

Exit JUDY.
JOEL sighs. Beat. JOEL sits down. Beat. He jumps back up,
with a realization.

JOEL
...Timmy! Timmy I THINK I FOUND IT!

JOEL runs off.

ACT ONE, SCENE 9

JUDY twirls onstage, looking happy and hopeful. She is in an unspecified part of town. BUBBA sits in a fold up beach chair by a trash can fire, playing his harmonica. He is dressed in an old beaten down sports coat and some patchwork long pants. JUDY stands before him, guitar case in hand. He looks up from his playing.

JUDY

Evening Bubba!

BUBBA

Heya Judy, how are things swingin' for my favorite gal?

JUDY
(Smiling broadly.)
Bubba, life is good.

BUBBA

Why don't you pull that ol' guitar out, and tell me all about it sis.

BUBBA pulls another fold out beach chair from behind his own and unfolds it as JUDY pulls her guitar out from its case. JUDY sets herself down next to BUBBA and they proceed to jam throughout the following conversation.

JUDY

Bubba, I do believe I fell in love tonight.

BUBBA

Is that so?

JUDY

It's true, it's true.

BUBBA

Who's the lucky guy?

JUDY

His name is Joel, he works at the barber shop downtown. He's the nicest and strangest person I think I've ever met.

BUBBA

Joel, huh? I think I've seen the kid around. Is he...

(BUBBA describes JOEL physically.)

JUDY

That's him! You know him?

BUBBA

I've seen him around, Seems like a nice kid, might have his head up in the clouds a little but... Well, there's nothing wrong with that, now is there?

BUBBA nods at JUDY and smiles, she smiles back and laughs. They trade solos for a few bars.

BUBBA (CONT'D)

So how long you two been going steady?

JUDY

Well, to be honest it's been kind of a whirlwind thing. We really just met a few days ago but... I don't know... I feel like I've been waiting for him all along.

BUBBA

Mmm...

They are quiet for a moment, the music slows and gets softer, fainter. JUDY begins to look a little preoccupied. She looks to BUBBA.

JUDY

Bubba... he wants me to come stay with him.

BUBBA

Is that so?

JUDY
(Almost not believing it herself.)

Yeah. It is.

Their music comes to a stop.

BUBBA

Well, that's great!

JUDY

It is great. It is...

BUBBA

I have to say, out of all of us down on our luck out here, and I include myself when I say that, I'm glad it's you that caught a lucky break. Lord knows, you deserve it after all you've done for us.

JUDY

Oh Bubba.

> She smiles warmly at him, but her smile slowly fades as bad thoughts begin to spin in her mind. She stands and begins to pace.

JUDY (CONT'D)

Bubba... I don't know if I can go with him.

BUBBA

Hmm?

JUDY

I... I don't know, I just...

> Her fears come spilling to the surface all at once, like boiling water bubbling out of a pot.

JUDY (CONT'D)

What if this is a mistake? I mean I've only met him, this is crazy! I mean, I love him but what if it doesn't last? What if he didn't mean it? What if he throws me out on the street again? Bubba, I don't think I could handle that.

BUBBA

Hey, sis, now don't go letting those bad thoughts get you all in a huff, huh? Just take a big ol' breath, breathe in-

>(She does.)

-and out.

>(She does.)

Now look. There's a million "What ifs" out there, and I know they've got to be running through your mind right now. That's ok, it's alright to not be sure of the future, that's just human nature sis. What matters though is the answer to one little question, and it's as simple as this.

>(Beat.)

Do you love him?

JUDY

I-

BUBBA

>(Interrupting.)

Before you answer, think about it. I mean really think, sis. If it really is love... then you'll know. Think about it.

>There is silence for a few moments as Judy runs through everything in her mind. She looks nervous at first, but her anxiousness slowly turns into a quiet, pleased resolve. As she thinks, an instrumental version of "I Love You" sneaks its way onto the scene.

JUDY

I know, Bubba... I know it's love.

>BUBBA spreads his arms.

BUBBA

That's all you really need.

>JUDY jumps up and hugs BUBBA.

JUDY

I'm gonna miss you, Bubba.

BUBBA

Oh, sis. I'll still be around. I know you're not gonna forget about us all. You got too big a heart for that.

(She smiles.)

You tell the others yet?

JUDY

Not yet, I'm making my way around town tonight. Speaking of which...

(She glances at her watch.)

I should probably get back to it. Got a lot of people to say "Bye" to.

BUBBA

(Winking.)

Let 'em down easy, sis.

JUDY

(Winking back.)

Only way I know how.

JUDY goes to put her guitar back in its case.

BUBBA

Now I know you've got to make your rounds, say your goodbyes, but you be careful out there tonight. It's a cold one and you know how these dark streets can be.

JUDY

Oh don't worry about me, I've got my love to keep me warm.

She stands to go.

BUBBA

Be good, sis.

She's smiling, but it's plain to see that she's holding back tears.

JUDY

Goodbye, Bubba.

> JUDY exits, stopping once to look back. BUBBA sits back
> down and plays a quiet little tune on his harmonica as she
> goes.

8. QUARTET

JUDY (CONT'D)
COULD THIS BE EVERYTHING I'VE DREAMED ABOUT?
JUDY'S PLACE IN PARADISE?
NOT EVERY GIRL WAS OFFERED A NEW LIFE TODAY
I COULD CARE ABOUT A DIFFERENCE HERE
OR I COULD GIVE UP THE GHOST
IF I GO WOULD I FORGET MY REASONS HERE
OR WOULD I FIND THE THING
A PERSON NEEDS THE MOST
THEY SAY IT'S COLD OUTSIDE, BUT I DON'T THINK I FEEL IT
IT'S CHILLY SOMEWHERE ELSE, BUT NOT RIGHT HERE
I GOT SOMETHING AND I CANNOT CONCEAL IT
IN THREE SHORT WORDS
IN THREE SHORT WORDS, MY TROUBLES DISAPPEAR
TAKE ME FAR BEYOND MY WILDEST DREAMS
WITH A NEW OPPORTUNITY
EVERY STEP OPENS UP A RAY OF SUNSHINE
EVERY BREATH IS WHAT I THOUGHT I'D NEVER BE
I CAN'T SOLVE THE PROBLEMS OF THE WORLD
OR EVEN BARELY ON THIS STREET
BUT I KNOW ONE THING: THERE WON'T BE ANYTHING
MORE PERFECT THAN THE GUY
WHO MAKES EVERYTHING COMPLETE
THEY SAY IT'S COLD OUTSIDE, BUT I DON'T THINK I FEEL IT
IT'S CHILLY SOMEWHERE ELSE, BUT NOT RIGHT HERE
I GOT SOMETHING AND I CANNOT CONCEAL IT
IN THREE SHORT WORDS
IN THREE SHORT WORDS, MY TROUBLES DISAPPEAR

> BILL sits in the barber shop waiting for JOEL. The door opens
> and he stands up.

BILL

Hey, Joel I...

TIMMY walks in.

BILL (CONT'D)

Oh... Timmy. Hey...

TIMMY

Hey Mr. McCale. I found Joel.

BILL

That's great! Where is he?

TIMMY

Well, I don't know. But I do know that he's doing something very important to him.

BILL

Ah. Apparently more important than getting home tonight.

TIMMY

Any other time, you know he would be here for you-

BILL

Here for me? I'm starting to think Joel could give a damn.

TIMMY
(Still kind of timidly.)
Hey, you...you don't have to be so hard on him you know.

BILL

What difference does it make if he's somewhere else?

TIMMY

He'll come back. You know he's coming back!

(Ad lib.)

64

BILL
(Cutting him off.)
I GIVE EVERYTHING TO HIM
HIS LIFE, HIS WORK, AND HOW DOES HE REPAY ME?
I WRAPPED A LIFETIME FORGED IN GOLD
AND PLACED IT IN THE CENTER OF HIS HAND
I VERY CAREFULLY PREPARED HIM FOR THE MOMENT HE'D CUT
HAIR
AND OVERTAKE ME
THE CHANCE OF A LIFETIME
AND HE'S THROWING AWAY EVERYTHING WE'VE PLANNED

TIMMY
I don't mean to intrude or anything, but he's got to look out for himself sometime.

BILL
What's that supposed to mean?

TIMMY
I just mean Joel's gotta figure out some stuff on his own. He's not going to ever learn how to deal with things if you plot the course of his life yourself. You can't be hovering over his shoulder forever.

BILL looks on sternly, displeased

TIMMY (CONT'D)
I'm sorry, it's really not my place.

(Beat. Then, under his breath:)
I just think he's having a rough time is all.

BILL
It's irresponsible, it's unnecessary, there's no reason why he needs to keep displacing his concerns in these developments or pursuing this girl. It's no way to make a living!

TIMMY
(To himself at first.)
YOU KNOW ITS NOT JUST YOUR LIFE
YOU'VE BEEN LIVING, YOU'RE JUST SWALLOWING HIS FUTURE
HE'S TRYING TO FIND HIMSELF NOW
AND HE'S GOT TO MAKE HIS MIND UP ON HIS OWN

BILL

What was that?

TIMMY
(Now to BILL, sort of pleading.)
HE HASN'T HAD THE CHANCE TO SEE
LIFE HAS MORE OPPORTUNITY
THAN HE'S BEEN GIVEN
HE'S NEVER SEEN BEYOND THE DOORS
THAN JUST THIS SIMPLE WAY TO LIVE THAT HE HAD KNOWN

BILL

I DON'T NEED YOUR ADVICE

TIMMY

IT WORRIES ME YOU'D SAY THAT
WHEN YOU'VE KEPT HIM SO STIFLED YOU OUGHT TO GIVE HIM
LEEWAY

BILL

I THINK I'D KNOW BETTER HOW TO RAISE MY SON
HOW WOULD YOU THINK TO UNDERSTAND OR DARE TO TRY TO
MAKE DEMANDS

TIMMY

I DIDN'T MEAN TO
BUT WOULD IT KILL YOU JUST TO TRUST HIM
YOU KNOW HE WON'T BE GONE, HE'LL ONLY JUST BE GROWN

TIMMY exits the barbershop, leaving Bill.

BILL

PERHAPS THE BOY IS RIGHT, PERHAPS THIS FIGHT'S ALREADY
WON
WHAT GOOD'S A FATHER IF HE CANNOT LEARN TO TRUST HIS
SON?
AFTER ALL THE WORLD IS FULL OF FATHERS STRICKEN WITH
THIS FEAR BUT JOEL'S NOT THEIR SON THERE, HE'S MY SON
HERE

JOEL

JUDY I SWEAR
I CAN BE A HOME FOR YOU
I'LL FOLLOW YOU ANYWHERE YOU WANT ME TO

> Their voices converge into a quartet with JUDY. The music fades.

JUDY

DISAPPEAR...
DISAPPEAR...
DISAPPEAR...

Oh my god.

> Blackout.
> End of act one.

ACT TWO, SCENE 0

9. ENTR'ACTE

Spotlight up on BUBBA, still dressed in hobo regalia. He looks a bit worse for wear, and pulls a blanket close around his shoulders as he speaks. He appears to be addressing the audience, but speaks as if to another character.

BUBBA

Last night was cold for all us out here on the street, I swear it mighta been the coldest night I've ever seen in this town. That rain wet up everything, made it near impossible to get a fire going. I saw a lotta folks huddled up last night, barely hangin' on... but I didn't see her... not after she left. I sure hope ya'll find her, I truly do.

The rest of the lights come on, revealing a bustling scene of homeless people receiving aid from volunteers and police. Some lie on the ground swaddled in blankets, and some are being loaded onto stretchers. Among the throngs of the homeless we can see ALEX, CAROL, and DAVID. The lights reveal a policeman who was standing next to BUBBA, with a notebook in his hand, scribbling down notes from the interview.

OFFICER DAVE
(Closing the notebook.)
That should be enough information, thanks for your help. We're gonna get right on it, but after the freeze last night there's been a lot of missing person reports filed. We'll let you know if we see any development.

BUBBA

Thank you.

The policeman nods and turns away, BUBBA looks down at the Harmonica in his hands. Lights down.

ACT TWO, SCENE 1

Lights back up, now on the barber shop. CHARLIE walks onstage, dressed for cold weather. Left and heads towards the shop. She walks past the tree in which TIMMY sits, eyes fixed on the shop. She notices him up in his perch and stops before she enters his line of sight. She sneaks up right to the base of the tree before she makes her presence known.

CHARLIE

Don't you have someplace to be?

TIMMY startles and almost falls out of the tree. CHARLIE bursts out laughing.

CHARLIE (CONT'D)

I'm sorry, that was just too easy.

TIMMY

I guess that's what I get for spacing out so much.

CHARLIE

Gotta keep your head out of those clouds! What are you doing up in that tree anyway?

TIMMY

Actually, I was waiting for you to get to work.

CHARLIE

Whoa... stalk much?

TIMMY

No! No, it's not like that! I was just... I mean... I...

CHARLIE

Dude, I was totally kidding.

TIMMY

Ah! Of course!

They are smiling at each other when CHARLIE realizes that no one is talking.

CHARLIE

Hey, so were you alright with the freeze last night? I heard a lot of people's heat went out.

TIMMY

Yeah, it got pretty bad downtown, but my apartment ended up alright.

CHARLIE

Ok, good. I heard it hit the homeless pretty bad, I was gonna head down to the shelter after work and see if they need a hand.

TIMMY

Well, that is quite socially conscious of you.

CHARLIE

We're all people, just trying to get by, you know? So, what are you up to right now?

TIMMY

Oh, you know. Just sitting in a tree, you know... same old, same old.

CHARLIE

Well, I was thinking of getting some coffee before work...

TIMMY

Ah, it is the most important meal of the day.

CHARLIE

What, coffee?

TIMMY

Yes?

The couple's eyes trace a jogger trotting across the stage, punctuating the silence.

TIMMY (CONT'D)

You meeting anyone?

CHARLIE

Nope, just flying solo... Alone... with no one to go with...

TIMMY

Well... maybe... if you wouldn't mind something new...

CHARLIE

Yes?

TIMMY

Maybe... You could try that new bagel place down on 3rd street.

CHARLIE is visibly disappointed.

CHARLIE

Oh. Yeah, I've heard they're pretty good.

TIMMY

Definitely worth a look...

Beat.

CHARLIE

Well, I'm gonna get going. Thanks for the recommendation. I'll see you around, Timmy.

She begins to walk by.

TIMMY

Charlie...

CHARLIE

Yeah?

10. AN HOUR WITH YOU (I JUST WANNA SAY)

TIMMY

I JUST WANNA SAY
I THINK YOUR
...SHOES LOOK NEAT

CHARLIE

What?

TIMMY

I mean...
I JUST WANNA SAY
I THINK YOU'RE
PRETTY SWEET
BUT I CAN'T HELP THE FEELING
YOU THINK I'M AN OK GUY
OR MAYBE I'M JUST CRAZY
Uh, never mind.

TIMMY turns around, making to awkwardly walk away.
CHARLIE has a moderately incredulous or confused
expression, but doesn't move a muscle. TIMMY pulls a
crumpled piece of paper from his pocket, double checking.

TIMMY (CONT'D)

I JUST WANNA SAY
YOU CUT HAIR...
PRETTY WELL

CHARLIE

I mean it's my job.

TIMMY

Let me finish...
I JUST WANNA SAY
I THINK YOU'RE
KIND OF SWELL
I'VE NEVER BEEN THAT HOT SHOT
THAT PLAYS THIS KIND OF GAME
BUT I DON'T THINK I'M CRAZY
TO THINK YOU FEEL THE SAME
AND I JUST WANNA SPEND AN HOUR WITH YOU
I JUST CAN'T STOP THINKING ABOUT ALL THE THINGS WE'D DO
I JUST WANNA SPEND AN HOUR WITH YOU
BUT I GUESS A COUPLE MINUTES STANDING HERE WITH YOU
WILL DO

CHARLIE

I JUST WANNA SAY

TIMMY

Hold on, I have a little more.

(Pause to read paper.)
Oh no, actually that was it sorry.

CHARLIE

I JUST WANNA SAY
I THINK YOUR "O"S ARE CUTE

TIMMY

What do you mean?

CHARLIE

When you sing!

TIMMY

Was I singing?!

CHARLIE

Ahem.
I JUST WANNA SAY

TIMMY

Wait.

The music stops. Pause.

TIMMY (CONT'D)
(All smiles.)
You think I'm cute?

CHARLIE

Do you shut up?

TIMMY
(Without missing a beat.)
I JUST WANNA SAY
I KNEW IT ALL ALONG
I JUST WANNA SAY
THERE'S NO WAY I'M EVER WRONG
AND I KNEW THROUGH THOSE WINDOWS
WHEN I WATCHED YOU FROM THIS TREE
YOU WERE PINING FOR ME BABY
STARING BACK AT ME

CHARLIE
I'm sorry, what?!

Beat.

TIMMY
What what?

CHARLIE
You really were stalking me?

TIMMY
I mean...let's not focus on that specifically.

CHARLIE crosses her arms.

TIMMY (CONT'D)
It's the highest form of flattery?

CHARLIE
(Playfully.)
I should go...

TIMMY
Wait! One last thing...

TIMMY rolls up his sleeves and walks to her, forcefully taking her hand. They dance a passionate tango. CHARLIE forces him away. TIMMY, disheartened, sits on the bench, a little bummed out. Finally, with a free moment to speak her mind...

CHARLIE

I JUST WANNA SAY
I NEVER WANTED THIS
I JUST WANNA SAY
YOU COULD HAVE JUST GONE
...FOR A KISS

> She gives TIMMY a quick peck on the lips. He's completely
> flabbergasted.

CHARLIE (CONT'D)

I'VE NEVER BEEN ROMANTIC
OR PURSUED BY ANYONE
BUT HOW COULD I AVOID THE GUY WHO JUST WANTS TO HAVE
FUN

TIMMY

I really like you, Charlie.

CHARLIE

(Laughing.)
I'VE ALWAYS KNOWN YOU DO

TIMMY

CAN WE HOLD HANDS TOGETHER

CHARLIE

FOR FOREVER?

CHARLIE AND TIMMY

ME AND YOU!
I JUST WANNA SPEND AN HOUR WITH YOU
TAKE A BREAK FROM EVERYTHING AND GET SOME TEA FOR TWO

TIMMY

MAYBE TAKE A STROLL OR SEE A ZOO

CHARLIE

HIKE TO THE NORTH POLE OR CURE THE FLU

TIMMY

CHANGE THE STATUS QUO OR STAGE A COUP

CHARLIE
(Slower.)
BUT MAYBE JUST SITTING HERE IS OK TOO

CHARLIE AND TIMMY
(Casually, out of tempo.)
I JUST WANT TO SPEND AN HOUR
WITH YOU

> CHARLIE rests her head on TIMMY's shoulder. ELLIE and
> RACHEL enter, ad lib "girl talk". CHARLIE, noticing, gives
> TIMMY a quick shove away. ELLIE and RACHEL don't notice.

ELLIE AND RACHEL
Hey Charlie!

CHARLIE
(A little shocked.)
Oh, hey.

ELLIE
We were just gonna get some coffee before work, want to come with?

CHARLIE
Yeah...sure thing.

> ELLIE, RACHEL, and CHARLIE leave, leaving a befuddled
> TIMMY onstage. After a moment, TIMMY picks himself up
> and walks off, confused and a little defeated.

ACT TWO, SCENE 2

Lights up on the barbershop. The chairs have been moved off to the side and there is a large card table set up in the center of the room. BILL and four of his friends, including MAC, sit playing poker.

BILL
(Setting his cards face up on the table.)
Read 'em and weep, boyos.

The losers around the table all groan. BILL rakes in a sizeable pile of chips.

MAC
Damn Bill, you're running hot tonight.

JENNY
(Throwing her cards on the table.)
Yeah, some guys have all the luck.

GARY
I think I saw him put that ace up his sleeve earlier!

BILL
Now, now, let's not start pointing fingers here. You know I won fair and square.

OLSEN
I had my eye on him the whole time, Gary. If you guys were smart like me, you'd have folded a long time ago.

JENNY
Oh, you're so right. Teach us how to be quitters like you, Olsen!

They all burst into laughter. BILL'S laughter turns into a coughing fit. After a bit, his friends notice.

GARY
Cripes, Bill. You okay?

BILL
Yeah... just fine... gimme a sec.

BILL takes a swig from a bottle of beer, and clears his throat one last time.

BILL (CONT'D)
(Slightly panting.)
See? Right as rain.

OLSEN
I'm telling you buddy, you should go see a doctor about that there cough.

BILL
Oh, I'm fine. Just a bit scratchy is all.

JENNY
Hell, you almost coughed up a lung a second ago. That seems a bit more than "scratchy" to me.

BILL
It's no worse than it has been for the past year and I've been managing fine so far. Why should I pay an arm and a leg to see a doctor who's just going to tell me the same thing they always do?

MAC
What? You get tired of hearing "Mr. McCale, you're old."?

BILL
Yes, actually. I'm not as used to hearing it as you are, old timer. Now are we gonna play cards or what?

OLSEN
Gary, Deal em'.

GARY passes five cards to each player at the table. They converse while he deals.

JENNY
So Mac. I'm gonna go ahead and ask you because I'm pretty sure we've all been thinkin' it... who does your hair?

MAC
Oh, this is the young Mr. McCale's handiwork. You like it? I'm trying to keep it fresh.

BILL

Joel did that?!

MAC

Yep, gave it to me on the house too!

GARY

Was that before or after he ran over your head with a lawnmower?

MAC

Har, har. You all laugh, but I know that you're jealous.

BILL
(Shaking his head.)

That boy...

OLSEN

He been acting up lately?

BILL

Not particularly. He just hasn't been around very much lately. He's missing work, missing school, when I do see him he barely says two words to me... He seems distracted. I'll take two.

GARY gives BILL two cards and takes the two that BILL set down. He does the same for the rest of the table when they ask.

OLSEN

Yeah, they get like that. I remember the time when my daughter locked herself up in her room. We had to make a little pulley system to get food up to her through the window. After a week, she snapped out of it and was prancing around the house, laughing and singin'. Never really found out what was wrong though. Three for me, Gary.

BILL

I don't think it's like that though. He's never been like this before.

MAC

Maybe he just needs a bit of space. You remember how we were as kids? Hell, we couldn't sit still for more than thirty seconds. Just one, Gare.

JENNY

That was a long time ago, things have changed since then Mac. Three please.

GARY

And two for the dealer.

BILL

Man... When did all that end up in the past? How has it been that long? I feel like if we go outside right now, we'll still be able to see the sign for the old burger place all lit up...

GARY

Oh man, they had the best malts at that place.

JENNY

Damn shame that they had to close it up.

OLSEN

I'll drink to that.

They all raise their bottles or glasses.

BILL

Here's to the old burger place... and to old friends.

They commence the clinking of glasses.

GARY

And here's to great haircuts!

They burst out laughing and clink glasses again. The lights go down as they resume playing and talking.

ACT TWO, SCENE 3

> Lights up. Townsfolk and hobos gather about the stage. It is now filled with customers. ELLIE, RACHEL, and CHARLIE are working in the shop. JOEL enters from stage left, and bursts into the shop.

ELLIE

Joel?!

JOEL

What? Oh, Hey Ellie.

ELLIE

Where have you been? We're totally swamped today!

JOEL

Awh Jeez, we really are, huh?

CHARLIE

Yeah, we are! So what are you waiting for? Take some of these customers, will you?

JOEL

I really wish I could stay to help but I'm just dropping by because I wanted to ask you guys something.

CHARLIE

Oh, come on Joel, you can't just bail and leave us like this!

JOEL

I'm sorry Charlie, I really am. But this is important.

CHARLIE
> (Sighing.)

Fine. What is it?

JOEL

I haven't seen Judy in an entire week, no one has. I'm really starting to get worried. You haven't seen her out around the shop at all have you?

RACHEL

Oh! I saw her with you last Monday!

CHARLIE, ELLIE, and JOEL look incredulously at RACHEL.

RACHEL (CONT'D)

...I guess you saw her then too...

ELLIE

Well, I haven't seen her.

CHARLIE

Neither have I.

JOEL

It was worth a shot. Thanks girls.

CHARLIE

You can't even stay for like an hour?

JOEL

I've gotta keep looking Charlie. I swear I'll make it up to you somehow.

JOEL goes to leave. His hand touches the doorknob and then...

CHARLIE

Joel!

He freezes, listening, but does not turn.

CHARLIE (CONT'D)

I hope you find her.

Without looking back, JOEL opens the door and leaves. Lights down on the barbershop as JOEL walks to a different part of town.

11. MISSING

JOEL

OH JUDY WHERE'D YOU GO?
I NEED TO KNOW
ONLY YOU COULD TAKE ME FROM THIS PLACE THIS PRISON.
I HAD EVERYTHING REDRAWN
BUT NOW YOU'RE GONE
AND NOW I CAN'T FIND MY WAY WHEN YOU'RE MISSING.
EVERYTHING WAS GOOD FOR US
JUST NOT SO LONG AGO
WHERE HAS THE WORLD TAKEN YOU
SOMEWHERE I COULD GO?
JUDY, JUDY, WHERE'S MY RAY
OF SUNSHINE, I NEED
TO KNOW

> JOEL moves toward the park where a few pedestrians are. We
> also see DAVID and CAROL meandering about stage, looking
> for handouts. On the bench lies a figure wrapped and
> swaddled in a blanket. The figure doesn't take up the whole
> bench, leaving space at the end of the bench. JOEL
> approaches a woman with a child.

JOEL (CONT'D)
Excuse me ma'am, I'm looking for a girl. She's about this tall, carries a
guitar around and-

MOTHER
(Rushing by him.)
Don't make eye contact, honey.

JOEL
Wait! I'm just trying to... OK, bye.

> JOEL moves on to a random PEDESTRIAN.

JOEL (CONT'D)
Sir! I'm looking for a missing girl, have you seen her? She's about this
tall,

(Goes on to describe JUDY EXTENSIVELY.)

PEDESTRIAN
(Interrupting JOEL'S rant.)
Hey, look man. If I give you my wallet, will you shut up?

JOEL
What? No, I just want to know if you've seen-

PEDESTRIAN
Here. Just take it. TAKE IT.

The PEDESTRIAN throws their wallet at him and runs. JOEL
plops down on the bench in frustration.

CHORUS
WHERE IS JUDY
I NEED TO KNOW
WHERE IS JUDY
I NEED TO KNOW
WHERE IS JUDY
I NEED TO KNOW
WHERE IS JUDY
I NEED TO KNOW

JOEL
NOTHING REALLY MATTERS TO ME
WHEN YOU'RE NOT AROUND
IT'S A COLD NIGHT WITH THE
BEATING SUN STILL ON THE GROUND

ALL
HERE THE WORLD IS CRUMBLING
UNTIL YOUR SPIRIT'S FOUND
I'LL KEEP LOOKING EVERYWHERE
JUDY I WON'T LET YOU

JOEL
DOWN

ALL
AHHH

Four POLICE OFFICERS enter from where the PEDESTRIAN
exits.

84

OFFICER DAVE

Son, are you Joel McCale?

JOEL

Um, yes sir. That's me.

OFFICER FRANK

We were told that you'd be somewhere out here. Your friend Charlie said to look for the guy who's probably harassing strangers for information.

JOEL

Oh, well that was just-

OFFICER DENNIS

Kid, we'll do the talking here OK?

OFFICER NANCY

Yeah. We're police officers. Let us do our job.

JOEL

Ok... how can I help you?

OFFICER DAVE

We've come to you regarding the missing persons report you filed on one... Judy... You didn't list a last name?

JOEL

Yes! Did you find her?

> The OFFICERS look at each other nervously. One them takes out a pitch pipe and plays a note.

12. REAL BAD NEWS

POLICEMEN
(A la "barbershop quartet")
JOEL WE GOTTA TELL YOU
WE'VE GOT REAL BAD NEWS
REGARDING YOUR MISSING HOMELESS BELL
ALL WE'VE FOUND OF JUDY
IS THESE TORN UP SHOES
SO WE BROUGHT THEM TO YOU JUST AS WELL
THIS SORT OF THING HAPPENS EVERY NOW AND THEN
WE'RE AFRAID THERE'S NO REAL POINT TO SEARCH AGAIN
THERE'S A CHANCE SHE'S OUT THERE BUT IT'S KIND OF SLIM
THERE'S REALLY NO HOPE
SORRY 'BOUT YOUR GIRLFRIEND
WE KNOW IT'S REAL SAD
THINKIN' ABOUT ALL THE GREAT OLD TIMES YOU HAD
AT LEAST YOU STILL HAVE YOUR DAD
HE'S NOT GOING
ANYWHERE

JOEL
Oh God...

OFFICER NANCY
You... gonna be alright kid?

JOEL
Yeah... yeah I'll be fine. Thank you officers. I'm sorry to take up your time.

The POLICEMEN exit.

ACT TWO, SCENE 4

13. FALLOUT

JOEL wanders about the stage, seeming to have lost purpose. He moves over toward the bench and plops himself down next to the lump on the bench. He sighs heavily as he sits, and the figure sits up suddenly and we see that ALEX was the figure.

JOEL

Holy-

ALEX

WHOA!

The two leap away from each other, JOEL jumping to his feet and ALEX scrambling over the edge of the bench. DAVID and CAROL come scrambling to the commotion.

CAROL

Alex! What's up?

DAVID

Yeah, man what's wrong?

ALEX
(From the ground.)
This guy just scared the stuffing outta me!

JOEL

I-I'm sorry, I didn't even see you there.

DAVID

Jeez, Alex, you shouted like bloody murder over here.

CAROL

Yeah, I thought you were getting dragged off by the cops or something.

ALEX

No, I'm fine, this guy here just-

He begins to recognize JOEL.

ALEX (CONT'D)

Wait a minute, you look familiar...

JOEL

Oh, no you must be thinking of someone-

CAROL

No, he's definitely right. We've seen you somewhere, I'm positive.

> ALEX gets up off the ground, and the three of them walk slowly towards him, encircling JOEL. They aren't threatening in their demeanor, but JOEL is clearly uncomfortable with the situation.

DAVID

Yeah, he's got one of those faces...

ALEX

Definitely.

CAROL

You from downtown, kid?

JOEL

No, I-

ALEX

What about near the outskirts of town, ever find yourself out there?

JOEL

I should probably be going-

> JOEL moves to leave.

DAVID

WAIT! I got it! You're that barber kid, ah?

CAROL

That's it! I knew we'd seen you around!

ALEX

Your dad's a real piece of work, isn't he?

JOEL

Well, he can be tough to get along with.

DAVID

To say the least!

ALEX

He threw a broom at me like a javelin once.

JOEL

Seriously?

ALEX

Yeah! Well, wait... maybe that was a dream I had once.

DAVID

Don't mind him, he's got focus problems. What's your name kid?

JOEL

Uh...

CAROL

Look kid, if we wanted to hurt you, do you think we'd even be talking to you? We're all just trying to get by here.

> After a little bit.

JOEL

I'm Joel McCale.

DAVID

Joel, huh? Good strong name. I'm David Williamson.

CAROL

Carol, Carol Bryant.

ALEX

And I'm Alex, just Alex.

DAVID

So, Joel McCale: Barber Extraordinaire, what are you doing way out here?

JOEL

Actually, I'm looking for someone... a friend of mine.

ALEX

Ain't we all?

JOEL mouths "what?" in confusion.

CAROL

Grab some bench kid, let's hear your story.

They all crowd onto the bench, with JOEL in the middle.

JOEL

Well, I guess it all started a few weeks ago, when I met Judy...

DAVID

Judy! Pretty little thing, plays the guitar and sews?

JOEL

Yeah, that's her! You guys know her?

CAROL

Of course we know her! We all know Judy around here.

ALEX

She's a bit of a local legend. She fixes all of us up with some swanky homemade winter digs each year.

DAVID

She's sure gotten us through some rough times, yessir.

JOEL

That's her, that's definitely her! She's who I've been looking for! Have you guys seen her at all? Do you know where she might be?

The three VAGRANTS looks at each other.

DAVID

Sorry kid, we haven't seen Judy in a month.

JOEL

Then I guess those policemen were right...

CAROL

Policemen? Is she alright?

JOEL

I... don't know. No one has seen Judy for weeks and I filed a missing persons report but... nothing.

ALEX

You're serious?

CAROL

She's...gone?

JOEL is silent.

DAVID

Without Judy, I... I don't know if we'll make it through the winter. I mean this coat isn't gonna last much longer.

CAROL

And my windbreaker's seen too much wind for two lifetimes.

JOEL

What about the shelters? I'm sure they can help you guys out.

CAROL

Some of us, yeah, but even last year I saw kids without jackets out in the alleys.

ALEX

Judy has always been there for us, I don't know... I just don't know what we're gonna do without her help.

CAROL
(Comforting ALEX.)
We'll figure it out, kid, don't worry you'll see.

DAVID

Yeah, we'll get through it somehow.

JOEL

I'll do it. I'll fix your clothes.

> As the HOBOS sing, JOEL begins to sew clothing. A few
> homeless people begin to crowd around. He works as best he
> can, churning out some makeshift clothing.

HOBOS

I CAN'T BELIEVE WE'VE LOST HER
I CAN'T BELIEVE SHE'S GONE
MAYBE JOEL HAS PROMISE
MAYBE HE'LL MOVE ON

DAVID

JOEL WE FOUND SOME SCRAPS HERE TO HELP YOU WITH YOUR
TASK

ALEX

I THINK I MAY HAVE FOUND HER

> (JOEL looks, hopefully.)

AT THE BOTTOM OF MY FLASK

JOEL

OH JUDY WHERE'D YOU GO?
I NEED TO KNOW
ONLY YOU COULD TAKE ME FROM THIS PLACE
THIS PRISON

> RACHEL arrives on the scene, JOEL now sits on the park
> bench, sewing and mending frantically. A small line of
> homeless people with tattered rags in their arms has formed.

RACHEL

Joel? What are you doing?

JOEL

Rachel! I'm uh... sewing.

RACHEL

I can see that, but... why?

JOEL

Rach, you wouldn't believe how many people need clothes. I mean this group right here is just from the last thirty minutes alone.

> He holds up what he's been working on to examine it. It's a dress, or at least what's left of it. He's made a valiant effort to reconstruct it, but the garment is just a wreck.

RACHEL

Joel... do you actually know anything about sewing?

JOEL

No, I don't. I'm sort of learning as I go here.

RACHEL

You look like you may be in a bit over your head here Joel, why exactly are you doing this?

> JOEL hands the dress to a HOMELESS WOMAN in front of him. She gasps when she gets it.

HOMELESS WOMAN

My God! Thank you, thank you, thank you!

> The WOMAN hugs him and walks away beaming.

JOEL

That's why.

RACHEL

Look, what you're trying to do here is amazing, it really is... but Ellie is really sick today and we really need your help back at the shop. You can't just bail on us again Joel, it's not fair.

> JOEL takes a moment to think. The HOBOS get a bit restless. He turns to the crowd.

JOEL

I'm sorry guys, that's all I can do for today.

The HOBOS sigh and all but a few disperse slowly as RACHEL leads JOEL to the shop where the TRIO are and he begins working again.

BARBER TRIO
WE'VE BEEN WONDERING ABOUT JOEL
HE'S TAKEN A DARK TURN
WE HOPE HE CAN FIND HIS WAY
WITHOUT LEAVING BRIDGES BURNED
TAKE A LOOK AROUND YOU, JOEL
AND TAKE A MOMENT'S PAUSE

RACHEL
I THINK IT'S SO TRAGIC

BARBER TRIO
TO LOSE HER WITHOUT CAUSE

JOEL
OH JUDY WHERE'D YOU GO?
I NEED TO KNOW
ONLY YOU COULD TAKE ME FROM THIS PLACE THIS PRISON.

There is a break in the work, and the BARBERS take a moment to relax. BILL is still nowhere to be found.

CHARLIE
Whew, we barely made it through that one.

JOEL
Yeah, I guess you guys really did need me.

CHARLIE
Hey now, don't get cocky.

JOEL
(Jokingly.)
Whatever you say, boss lady.

TIMMY bursts through the door with a box.

JOEL (CONT'D)
(More relieved than excited.)
Timmy!

TIMMY

Good afternoon my barber-ing best friends. I come bearing doughnuts! Please, hold your applause! I shall need a moment to bask in your adoration!

> CHARLIE snags the box from him as he assumes a "basking position."

CHARLIE

Well aren't you just a gem.

TIMMY

Why, yes I am!

JOEL

Hey, throw one of those bad boys my way!

> CHARLIE takes a doughnut and passes the box off. The three of them sit down in the barber's chairs.

JOEL (CONT'D)

So, what have you been up to man?

TIMMY

Well, you won't believe it, but I got a job.

JOEL

Say it ain't so!

CHARLIE

No way! That's awesome Timmy!

JOEL

Now, who was crazy enough to hire a bum like you?

TIMMY

The doughnut shop! I made this batch myself!

JOEL

Whoa... really? These are pretty good dude.

TIMMY

I know right? It's weird, but... I actually kind of enjoy having a job.

JOEL
Who are you, and what have you done with Timmy?

TIMMY
I can scarcely believe it myself.

CHARLIE raises her doughnut into the air.

CHARLIE
A doughnut-toast to Timmy! And his new found work ethic!

They toast heartily.

CHARLIE (CONT'D)
Really though, Joel. Thanks for helping us out. We couldn't have done it without you.

JOEL
No problem. I'm sorry I haven't been here more often, it's just the whole Judy thing still has me down and now I'm helping to mend clothes for the homeless... it's been an interesting few weeks to say the least.

CHARLIE
How about this then. Timmy and I can close the shop up for the night so that you can go and mend clothes for a while.

JOEL
You guys would do that for me?

TIMMY
Of course dude, we've got your back!

CHARLIE
Go on. From what Rachel said, you've got your work cut out for you.

JOEL
Thanks guys. I really appreciate it.

JOEL runs out of the shop, leaving CHARLIE and TIMMY alone. They look at each other for a second.

CHARLIE

Jeez, I thought he'd never leave!

TIMMY

Me neither.

> TIMMY and CHARLIE kiss passionately. Lights up on the park
> where JOEL has returned to work for the HOMELESS.

VAGRANTS

I CAN'T BELIEVE WE'VE LOST HER
I CAN'T BELIEVE SHE'S GONE
MAYBE JOEL HAS PROMISE
MAYBE HE'LL MOVE ON

ALEX

JOEL WE'RE GETTING WORRIED

CAROL

OUR FEET ARE GETTING COLD

DAVID

HE CAN'T BE OUR JUDY

VAGRANTS

OR SPIN THREADS INTO GOLD

> When the hobos finish singing, only ALEX, CAROL, and
> DAVID remain with JOEL. JOEL holds up a pair of pants that
> don't look too terrible.

JOEL
(Handing them jackets.)

Here you go guys.

ALEX

Thank you, Joel.

JOEL

No problem.

DAVID

No, really Joel... Thank you.

DAVID and ALEX shake his hand, and CAROL hugs him.

JOEL

You guys stay warm out there, OK?

CAROL

We will now, thanks to you.

JOEL

Hey, you guys haven't seen my scissors, have you?

ALEX

Nope, sorry pal.

DAVID
(On his way offstage.)
Don't you work in a barber shop? You should have buckets of scissors to use.

JOEL

Touché.

Exeunt vagrants.
JOEL rushes over to the shop, unlocks it and enters. He looks around for a moment, then sees the golden shears up on the wall. He walks over to the wall where they hang and is taking them off the wall when BILL comes in through the front door.

JOEL (CONT'D)

Pop!

BILL

Joel, what are you doing? Charlie already closed up.

(He sees the shears in JOEL'S hands.)
And what are you planning on doing with the family shears?

JOEL

I... I need a pair of scissors.

BILL

Well, there's plenty of other ones around the shop. Why do you need those?

JOEL

I dunno, these were just the first ones I thought of. I just need some scissors.

BILL

What's your big scissor emergency, son?

      JOEL is silent for a moment.

JOEL

I need them to mend clothes.

BILL

So that's what you've been spending all your time doing? Sewing?

JOEL

Yes. For the homeless.

BILL

Joel, we've been busier than ever lately and you've just been off hanging out with deadbeats?!

JOEL

They're not deadbeats, pop! They're people, just like me and you.

BILL

They are deadbeats. And they clearly have your loyalty.

JOEL

No, it's not that simple pop!

BILL

Is it not? Everyone in town's talking about how you've been out there with them for days! And now you're going to use the family shears, which were passed down by my father's father, to cut up some strips of fabric?!

      BILL begins to cough uncontrollably.

JOEL

...Pop.

BILL

Joel, you've got to realize that I'm not going to be around forever, and I need to know that our legacy will continue. I've raised you to cut hair since you were six, I don't understand how you can suddenly care so little about what happens to the shop-

JOEL

(Shouting.)

My eyes are open Dad!

BILL is taken aback.

JOEL (CONT'D)

I care about the shop, I really do. And I care about you, pop. More than anything. But you've had me pegged for a barber since the second I could hold a razor. You trained me, you praised my work, and you built me into who I am today but never once did you ask if it was what I wanted. I've gone along with it for seventeen years now, never questioning, never wondering what else was out there. But Judy opened my eyes. She showed me that it doesn't matter what life sticks you with; you can always make your own way.

There is a long pause.

BILL

I think you should go.

JOEL

Pop, you don't understand!

BILL

I understand plain enough that you don't want to be here!

JOEL

What can I say to make you see?!

A guitar wails over JOEL and BILL as they engage in musical combat.

BILL

OH JOEL WHERE DID YOU GO?
I NEED TO KNOW
I NEED YOUR FOCUS HERE WITH ME

BILL	**JOEL**
WITH YOUR FAMILY	EVERYTHING IS DIFFERENT
I'VE CAREFULLY PREPARED	NOW
YOU	NOTHING LIKE BEFORE
FOR THE MOMENT YOU'D CUT	MY FUTURE FACES ME
HAIR	LIKE AN UNOPENED DOOR
AND OVERTAKE YOUR FATHER	
DEAREST	
IN A FEW SHORT WEEKS	
HOW COULD YOU DO THIS TO	
ME	
TO MY SHOP, AND TO YOUR	
FAMILY?	
OH WHEN WILL YOUR LIFE	
BEGIN?	

BILL AND JOEL
HERE THE WORLD IS CRUMBLING
TILL YOU LET ME IN
SO LET ME GO OR LET ME KNOW
WHEN WILL YOUR/MY LIFE BEGIN?

BILL
Give me those shears.

> JOEL complies. BILL takes them as JOEL leaves. BILL begins
> setting up the shop for poker night, he is livid. Sloppily
> throwing down chairs and setting the table up. He grows
> physically upset and seems to be on the edge of a breakdown.
> He is coughing uncontrollably now. BILL falls to his knees,
> coughing violently into his hands. ALEX and DAVID enter
> and notice him on the ground through the window. They
> rush into the shop to aid him. BILL continues his coughing
> fit.

ALEX
Hey old man, are you alright?

DAVID
He doesn't look too good. We gotta get him to a hospital.

They pull to his feet and carry him out, as the lights fade out. After a time, the lights flip on and we see JOEL standing next to the light switch.

JOEL

Pop?

After there is no response, JOEL begins to pick up the mess that BILL made setting up for poker the previous night. As he cleans, the phone begins to ring and JOEL answers it.

JOEL (CONT'D)

Hello, this is the McCale Family Barber Shop. We're closed.

DOCTOR DAVE

Yes, this is Doctor Dave, with Birchwood General. Is this Joel McCale?

JOEL

Yes, that's me.

DOCTOR DAVE

I'm calling about your father, Bill McCale.

JOEL

What's wrong? Is everything alright?

DOCTOR DAVE looks at his colleagues and one of them pulls out a pitch pipe, exactly like the policemen did.

14. REAL BAD NEWS (REPRISE)

DOCTORS

JOEL WE GOTTA TELL YOU
WE'VE GOT REAL BAD NEWS
REGARDING YOUR SICK OLD FATHER BILL
TURNS OUT WHAT HE HAS IS MORE THAN
JUST THE FLU
AND OUR CLINIC'S RUNNING OUT OF PILLS
THIS SORT OF THING HAPPENS EVERY NOW AND THEN-

> JOEL hangs up, slamming the phone down. Lights down on
> JOEL. The Doctors on the other side of the stage look at each
> other for a moment.

DOCTOR DAVE

Kid? You there?

DOCTOR NANCY

Was it something we said?

> Lights down.

ACT TWO, SCENE 5

>Lights come back up on the barbershop that afternoon. It is empty except for JOEL who is arranging various items or sweeping up. TIMMY wanders in, a large grin on his face.

TIMMY

Afternoon brother!

JOEL

Hey.

TIMMY

What's the word? Wait! I've got some breaking news right now! I kissed Charlie!

JOEL

Congratulations.

TIMMY

Man, I took your Dad's advice and boy did it pay off. I mean she doesn't really want to be seen in public with me or anything but still, it's something. Jeeze, Charlie is just so... so great!

JOEL

Dude, if you're gonna come in here and gush all over can you at least bring a mop and wipe up after?

TIMMY

Ouch, man. I thought you'd be happy for me. I finally have a shot.

JOEL
>(Sarcastically.)

Yeah, yeah, girl of your dreams, a loving family, a steady job. Everything I don't have. I couldn't be happier.

>TIMMY realizes they aren't goofing around and stops, looking anxiously at JOEL.

TIMMY

Are you alright?

JOEL

No.

TIMMY

Do you want to talk about it?

JOEL

Well who am I to ruin the mood?

TIMMY

Dude, what's your problem?

JOEL

My problem, dude, is that Judy is gone. My dad thinks I'm trying to destroy everything my family has worked for over generations, and there's no way to get out of the situation I've waltzed into without hurting someone. If I stay here, I fail the homeless who are counting on me. If I do what I want and help them, I fail my father. Things just can't go right anymore.

TIMMY

Joel, you can't think like that. You're just upset man. It's just like I've been saying at work--

JOEL

Just like you've been saying at work! That's exactly what I'm talking about. I'm not supposed to be the helpless loser here!

TIMMY stares at JOEL, incredulous and hurt.

JOEL (CONT'D)

I...I didn't mean it like that.

TIMMY

Then what did you mean, Joel?

JOEL

I just meant-

TIMMY

You just meant to suck some pity out of me. I'm trying to help and what to you do? You put me down.

JOEL

Listen, I have a lot going on that you can't wrap your head around!
You always think you've got it so bad. You need to stand up and quit
being such a little bitch!

JOEL

(Moving to leave.)
I don't have to deal with this.

TIMMY

I'M NOT DONE YET.

JOEL

THEN SPIT IT OUT.

TIMMY

YOU THINK YOU'VE GOT IT SO BAD, YOU NEED TO STEP BACK
AND
REALIZE-

JOEL

(Interrupting, amidst short bursts as TIMMY
attempts to interrupt.)
HOW CAN YOU UNDERSTAND? WHAT THE HELL DO YOU KNOW?
THIS IS MY
LIFE, WITH COMPLICATIONS YOU CAN'T EVEN IMAGINE, AND IF
YOU THINK YOU HAVE THE RIGHT TO-

(Ad lib until cut off by TIMMY.)

15. DO YOU REALIZE?

TIMMY
DO YOU THINK YOU'RE GETTING ANYWHERE
WITH THIS GLOOM THAT YOU'VE PUT ON ARE YOU WALLOWING
IN RAINCLOUDS
AND JUST WAITING FOR THE DAWN?
ARE YOU WHINING WHEN YOU COULD HAVE
FIXED THESE PROBLEMS ALL ALONG?
YOU KEEP THIS UP AND
EVERYONE YOU LOVE WILL SOON BE GONE!
DO YOU REALIZE THERE'S SOME OF US YOU'RE LEAVING HERE
BEHIND? THAT THERE'S CRIPPLING PROBABILITY THERE'S
SOMETHING MORE TO FIND?
THAT YOU'RE A FREAKING COWARD JUST FOR BEING SO
RESIGNED
SO LISTEN UP NOW, PAL, IT'S TIME YOU DIDN'T ACT SO BLIND!

JOEL
You're one to talk about cowardice! I remember you used to be too scared to cross the damn street without me.

TIMMY
I guess that's the thing about people, Joel. I guess sometimes they grow up.

(Cutting off an interjection from JOEL.)
You can ignore me all you want, but I'm not the one slooping around by himself like a lonely asshole.

JOEL
You know what, I don't have to put up with this.

JOEL pushes through the barbershop door.

TIMMY
Oh no, we're not through here.

TIMMY follows through the door as the shop closes up to reveal the outside in a dynamic and powerful expensive technical display simulating a camera circling around. The argument continues outside.

TIMMY (CONT'D)

I HAVE KNOWN YOU SIXTEEN YEARS NOW
AND YOU'VE GOT TO TAKE A HINT HOW CAN YOU THINK YOU'D UNDERSTAND
WHAT GROWING OLDER MEANT?
OH, HOW CAN YOU BE HAPPY WHEN YOU'RE BEING SO DAMN BENT?
WELL TAKE A SIDE WITH ME OR SADNESS MY PATIENT'S RATHER SPENT
Now what do you have to say for yourself?

JOEL

You can talk all you want, you still don't understand!

TIMMY

OH EVERYTHING YOU KNOW IS MADNESS
YOU THINK I CANT UNDERSTAND THIS
PASSING STRANGE DISMAY
OH YOU ARE SURE THE WORLD IS ENDING
WHINING ON YOUR OWN, PRETENDING
THINGS CANT GO YOUR WAY
DO YOU REALIZE ITS NOT ABOUT WHATS ONLY TROUBLING YOU
THAT THERES PEOPLE YOURE SURROUNDED BY WHO NEED
THEIR BEST FRIEND TOO
THAT IF YOU CLOSE OFF THE OUTSIDE
YOU'LL FORGET WHAT YOU ONCE KNEW?
DON'T PUSH ME OUT JOEL
HEY, HEY I'M TALKING TO YOU

DO YOU REALIZE THAT MAYBE YOU ARE NOT THE ONLY ONE?
THAT MAYBE PEOPLE CARE ABOUT YOU, BARBER, BEST FRIEND, SON.
THAT MAYBE YOU SHOULD STAY AND TRY, NOT ALWAYS TRY TO RUN. I'LL WAIT FOR YOUR UNDERSTANDING, UNTIL THEN I'M DONE
DONE
DONE
OHHH I'M DONE

> TIMMY exits. Leaving JOEL alone on the empty stage. Overcome with anger, he deals the barber pole a swift kick, and it flickers out. The stage grows dark, but not so dark that we can't see JOEL clamber down the stage.

ACT TWO, SCENE 6

> JOEL is alone on a large, empty, dark stage.

JOEL
(Defeated.)

Damn.

> In silence, he clambers down to the front of the stage as a screen/curtain drops below him to conceal the shop. He settles down alone and begins to sing timidly to himself.

16. I LOVE YOU (REPRISE)

JOEL (CONT'D)

I LOVE YOU
EVEN THOUGH YOU ARE HOMELESS

> While he sings, the vagrants and BUBBA enter quietly behind him with looks of gentle concern. JOEL does not notice.

JOEL (CONT'D)

MORE THAN MANY, MAYBE ANY
TREASURES IN THE SKY

BUBBA AND JOEL

WHILE YOU'RE WITH ME

JOEL

Oh, I didn't realize you were...hey, hey guys.

BUBBA

I'm sorry, we've never been formally introduced.

JOEL

Joel. I'm Joel.

BUBBA

Yeah, I know who you are.

> JOEL tilts his head in confusion.

BUBBA (CONT'D)

I'm a friend of Judy's.

JOEL

Yeah, well that's over now.

BUBBA

Sounds like you've got a story to tell, kid. Why don't you take a load off and tell ol' Bubba what's on your mind?

JOEL

Really?

BUBBA

Sure! We got nowhere to be.

JOEL

Well...I work in a barbershop...
Worked in a barbershop. With my pop.

CAROL

We've been acquainted.

BUBBA

(Like a mild, fatherly snapping turtle.)

Hush!

JOEL

And he wants me to keep in the family business. You know, pass on the tradition. But then I met Judy and everything turned upside-down. Can I speak candidly?

VAGRANTS AND BUBBA

Of course!

JOEL

We were so...in love. Everything lined up, like it was just for me. And in a second it vanished. Judy was...gone. And everything went to hell.

BUBBA

And that's the whole story?

JOEL

Well, no. She showed me how much I loved helping people. I mean I always have, but everything was just so much more vivid this way, you know? But that never lasts. I couldn't hack it. And now Pop's sick and my best friend can't bear to be around me, and everything's just kind of...empty.

BUBBA

Empty?

JOEL

I have nothing left.

> JOEL puts his head in his hands. BUBBA watches him for a moment before speaking.

BUBBA

Son, I want you to listen to what you just said and think about who you're talking to you when you say you got nothin' left. I sleep on a bench. I can't sit near the curb for fear of gettin' in folks' way. You know the other day a little girl walked by with her mother, just came from that balloon cart down the street. She got distracted for just a second and her balloon managed to wander off into that tree over yonder. I, acting like the gentleman I thought I was took it upon myself to retrieve it for her, but as I turned around to hand it to this little girl do you know what she did? She started crying. Couldn't have been any older than six, and just the sight of me put her in tears. So you can tell me about hard times, but don't come to me with "I got nothin' left". Because I still got somethin' left. I got somethin' and he got somethin' and you, boy, I'm sure you got somethin' left. All you have to do is go out and get it. No one can decide what you've got but you.

JOEL

Hah, sounds like something Timmy would say.

BUBBA

Timmy?

JOEL

Yeah, my friend. At least he used to be.

BUBBA

And you're letting him run off too?

111

JOEL

It's my problem, I have to figure this out alone.

BUBBA

Now what on earth makes you think that?

JOEL

Well that's what they say.

BUBBA

Huh. That's what they say.

17. STARTING TO FEEL SOMETHING

BUBBA (CONT'D)

I've heard a lot of things from a lot of people, telling me how to solve what's wrong with me and what's wrong with where we are and what we're doing. You're right: they say "it's your problem, you better do this alone." They say keep working your sorry little behind off because it'll all turn out in the end. You waste your breath telling me "they say" this or that, I've been there before. They say wait. Be good.
THEY SAY HOLD ON
AND PATIENCE IS A VIRTUE
BUT PATIENCE I LOST LONG AGO
SO WHAT FOR
THIS WEARY TRAVELER
TO HOLD UP HIS HEAD
WHEN HE'S GOT NOTHING TO WAIT FOR ANYMORE?
WHEN NOTHING GETS INSIDE YOU
AND NOTHING REALLY MATTERS
SATISFACTION, YOU DON'T KNOW WHERE IT'S BEEN
JUST LOOK INTO THE SUNSET
SEE THE ROSE SUNLIGHT SCATTER
AND YOU'RE STARTING TO FEEL SOMETHING AGAIN

JOEL

I understand you're trying to help, but songs and sunsets don't fix the world.

BUBBA

Nothing fixes the world, kid. Besides, that's not your department.

JOEL

How is anything supposed to be right if nothing's fixable?

BUBBA

I never said that, did I? Some things come easy, some things take some work, and sometimes you just have to kick up your shoes and remember that where you're sitting is still somehow beautiful in its own way.

IT ALWAYS SEEMS TO START OUT
ONE CLEAR NOTE OF PASSION
WHEN EVERYTHING SEEMS TO SOUND THE SAME
IT THROWS YOU
AND SPINS YOU
AND IT HITS YOU SO CLEAN
LIKE A WHIRLWIND
LIKE A FREEFALL
LIKE THE RAIN
FLOWERS BY THE ROADSIDE
BLOWING BLOSSOMS DOWN THE STREET
SUMMER BREEZES ROLL THE SWEAT OFF YOUR CHIN
A BRIGHT BLUEBIRD SINGS A MELODY
THAT FILLS YOUR EARS SO SWEET
AND YOU'RE STARTING TO FEEL SOMETHING AGAIN
NO YOU CAN'T PREDICT THE FUTURE
YOU KNOW THIS AIN'T NOTHING NEW
BUT TAKE ONE LITTLE MOMENT
AND LISTEN TO THE SIMPLE SONG
OF STARTS GROWING NEARER
AND DAYS GETTING CLEARER
AND MOONLIGHT
SPELLING OUT GOOD FORTUNE
THOUGH IT'S WRITTEN IN THE SAND
AND YOU'RE STARTING TO FEEL SOMETHING AGAIN
TAKE THAT TRIP TO SOMETHING AGAIN
STARTING TO FEEL SOMETHING AGAIN

JOEL

Bubba...I think I get it.

BUBBA

Then what are you wastin' time for? You still got something good left,
and you best be goin' out and keepin' it that way!

JOEL

You're right. I can make this right! Thanks Bubba! I won't forget this!

BUBBA

(Slyly.)
No, son, I know you won't.

JOEL rushes off. Exeunt vagrants and BUBBA.

ACT TWO, SCENE 7

> TIMMY and CHARLIE stand together, discussing something or other. JOEL enters, excited and clearly out of breath.

JOEL
Timmy! Timmy! I have to talk to you!

TIMMY
(To CHARLIE.)
Oh great, what does he want?

JOEL
(Sounding more excited than remorseful.)
Timmy, I was wrong. Everything you said was completely right! I'm sorry. You were right!

TIMMY
(To CHARLIE.)
Would you please tell Joel here that if he wants to apologize he's gonna want to sound a little more sincere?

CHARLIE
(Interrupting him.)
No, we're not playing this game.

> CHARLIE turns TIMMY around to face JOEL.

JOEL
(Taking a moment to pause.)
Timmy, I'm really sorry. I really meant it. You've been right from the start and I should have listened to you all along. Can you forgive me?

TIMMY
No, dude. You're a dick!

> CHARLIE, in the same fashion as before, turns TIMMY again to face her in an aside.

CHARLIE
(To JOEL.)
Give us a minute, thanks.

(To TIMMY.)
Listen, I know you guys had a falling out and what have you, but you and Joel are tighter than that and you should give him a chance.

TIMMY
Hell no, he's just going to turn around and stomp all over me again.

CHARLIE
You don't know that! He sounds really sincere, Timmy.

TIMMY
I swear on all that is good and holy there is absolutely, definitely zero percent chance of me forgiving-

CHARLIE
I'll go on a real date with you.

TIMMY
(Instantly turning around.)
Jo-el, I've carefully considered my options and I think it's in the interest of friendship that I forgive you.

JOEL laughs at TIMMY's maneuver and stretches out his hand, smiling warmly.

JOEL
...Brothers?

TIMMY resumes his serious demeanor, as if remembering his feud with JOEL. He tries his best to skewer JOEL with a begrudging look, but his frown slowly softens.

TIMMY
Brothers.

CHARLIE
So what's next for you then, Joel? Are you coming back to the shop?

JOEL

Not quite. I was wandering downtown not but a few minutes ago and talked with some really incredible people

TIMMY

Careful, dude, you're starting to sound a little inspired.

JOEL

Charlie, I need you to take over the shop.

CHARLIE

Me? But I don't-

JOEL

Don't even start, you're the one who always comes on time, keeps inventory, and cuts the cleanest. I mean, you saw what I did to Mac, right?

CHARLIE

I don't know what to say, Joel.

JOEL

For now? Don't say anything. But you'd better go get some sleep if you're gonna open tomorrow. And if you still don't know what to say then, I always like starting with "good morning Monday".

> CHARLIE, stunned, kisses JOEL on the cheek, then runs over to do the same to TIMMY, but TIMMY swiftly spins her into a dip and gives her a deep, passionate kiss. CHARLIE begins to run off, glances back at TIMMY lovingly, and continues off.

TIMMY
(Eyes still on the space where CHARLIE was.)

Wow.

JOEL

Snap out of it, dude. We have work to do if we're gonna open next week.

TIMMY

If we're gonna open next week?

JOEL

Yeah, listen up, I have a business proposition. You know that lot
down the street from the barbershop?

TIMMY

Yeah, I know it.

JOEL

Let's just say we're gonna have to build a little more before this show
is on the road. Come on, I'll explain on the way!

JOEL and TIMMY exit.

18. GOOD MORNING MONDAY (BARBERSHOP TALES REPRISE)

Spotlight on the COPS/DOCTORS quartet opposite them as
the curtain rises to reveal the old barbershop set, now
transformed into a new establishment. The tree is replaced
by a balloon stand. The new shop sign is covered by a tarp,
and inside we see a collection of odds and ends, clothing
creatively upcycled from other materials. At the center hangs
the suit and cap BUBBA wore in the opening prologue. A big
red ribbon is strewn across the front.

POLICEMEN/DOCTORS

GOOD MORNING MONDAY, MY FAVORITE TIME
THE DAY THAT STARTS OFF EVERY WEEK
NOBODY KNOWS WHAT WE'RE GONNA FIND
BUT WE KNOW IT'LL BE UNIQUE
SWOON WITH ME IN SUNRISE, MY VALENTINE,
AND LET BEFORETIME SLIP AWAY
NOTHING SWEETER OR MORE DIVINE
ANOTHER START TO ANOTHER DAY

Throughout, characters passing by on the street respond to
"good morning Monday" with a cheerfully spoken "good
morning Monday!" in return.

SHE-VAGRANTS

GOOD MORNING MONDAY, MY FAVORITE TIME
IT'S WHEN WE STOP LOOKING OH SO DRAB
WE GET OUR CLOTHES WHEN WE WAIT IN LINE

118

FABULOUS SHE-VAGRANT 1
This fashion's, dare I say it, FAB!

BARBER TRIO
GOOD MORNING MONDAY, WE GOT THE SHOP
AND NOW THIS BRAND NEW BUSINESS TOO
LIKE SOMETHING'S STARTING THAT JUST CAN'T BE STOPPED
GOOD MORNING MONDAY TO YOU TOO!

> Spotlight on JOEL, on a scaffold next to the newly cloaked building. The music backs off to reveal a tender yet steadily intensifying moment. As the music builds, JOEL pulls away the veil to reveal the sign, which says "Judy's Fine Eveningwear Boutique".

JOEL

CAN'T KEEP GRIEVING
I BELIEVE IN
BREAKING FROM MY STRIFE
IT'S MY DUTY
TO YOU JUDY
SOMETHING MORE THAN LIFE
SOMETHING MORE THAN LIFE
JOEL AND THE BARBER TRIO
JUDY'S FINE EVENINGWEAR BOUTIQUE
THE YEAH YOU BETTER GET IN LINE EVENINGWEAR BOUTIQUE
THE ONLY SIMPLY DIVINE EVENINGWEAR BOUTIQUE
YOU BETTER COME BY OUR WAY
EVERY DAY

CHARLIE
MY HEAD IS SPINNING, I DON'T KNOW WHAT'S UP
BUT YOU KNOW I WILL TAKE THE CHANCE
IT'S ABOUT TIME I STARTED MOVIN' UP OR MAYBE MOVIN' INTO
ROMANCE

TIMMY
(To Joel.)
NOW LET'S BORROW
FROM TOMORROW
EVERYTHING WE NEED
I'M NOT MESSING
I'M PROFESSING
BROTHERS WILL SUCCEED!

119

Dance break!

JOEL/ALL
COULD THIS BE MY/YOUR DESTINY
BEFORE MY/YOUR VERY EYES?
FOUND THE FASHION OF MY/YOUR PASSION
SING IT TO THE SKIES
SING IT TO THE SKIES

> Lights and smoke explode on top of Judy's Fine Eveningwear
> Boutique, revealing the angelic whiteclad GHOST OF JUDY,
> wind blowing through her hair, wailing on the guitar soloing
> over "I Love You" as a lit cigarette dangles from her lips. Joel
> shows her some sign of reverence.

JOEL AND JUDY
WHILE OUR LOVE LIVES
WE CAN NEVER BE HOMELESS

> In front of the big finish musical chaos, BILL steps out from
> behind the crowd with the help of a cane. He looks older and
> moves a little slower, but with purpose. He holds a small
> brown box under his arm.

BILL
Joel?

TIMMY
(Quietly.)
Hey pop.

BILL
I heard there was some sort of commotion going on at the lot next to
the shop, but I have to say I didn't expect all this.

JOEL
Well you missed the big reveal, but we haven't technically done the
grand opening yet.

BILL
(Nodding.)
Right, right.

> A member of the crowd coughs.

120

BILL (CONT'D)
(Quickly.)

That's pretty nice workmanship on the sign there though. Did you do that yourself?

JOEL

Oh yeah, Timmy and I did it. Mac lent us some equipment, we just sort of hammered it out.

BILL

Did you now? Looks pretty professional. Nice, crisp lettering, looks pretty level. Good job, kid.

JOEL
(Smiling nervously.)

Thanks pop, it was really nothing...

> They both look at the ground for a moment. The rest of the cast looks on in anticipation.

JOEL (CONT'D)

Pop, look. I know I haven't really been around when you needed me lately, and I know that things have been hard for us...
You raised me to believe in hard work, to believe that if I had a dream I could make it a reality with my own hands. That's what I'm doing here, what I'm doing now. And even though it might seem to you that I've forgotten everything you taught me--

BILL
(Interrupting JOEL.)

Son...

> BILL looks sincerely at JOEL for a moment before turning and looking out over the audience, as if he were looking out over the whole town.

BILL (CONT'D)

You know, it's all too easy to forget that once there was nothing but trees and rocks right here where we're standing. That was around the time my great, great grandpop was alive. They had to clear this whole area of forest before they could build on the land and in fact, some of the buildings in town are made from the wood of those trees, including our shop. I know that because my father told me, as his father told him, as his father before him knew because he was there when it happened. Our family legacy is embedded in the grain of this lumber, Joel. I guess I just always thought you would go about making yours the same way we did and for a while, well, that broke my heart. But I look at this old shop now and I see the faces gathered around it, new and old, rich and poor, and I can't help but feel like... like I might have been wrong. You've created something new for yourself here, kid. And even though it's something I might not be able to fully understand... I have to say I've never been more proud of you in my life.

> They embrace. BILL wipes a tear from his eye as he takes the box from under his arm and presents it to JOEL.

BILL (CONT'D)

And kid, if the things I've taught you made it so you could do this in a few days, well, I can't wait to see what you'll be able to do in a lifetime.

> BILL hands the box to JOEL. JOEL looks down confused.

JOEL

What's this?

> JOEL opens the box and reaches in, pulling out the golden shears.

BILL

I just figured you could probably use some new scissors.

19. FINALE

JOEL

Pop...I-

BILL

No buts, they're yours now and it looks like you've got a lot of work ahead of you today, kid, so how about we get this show on the road?

JOEL

(Beaming.)

I'd like nothing more.

> Together JOEL and BILL use the golden shears to cut the ribbon from the front of the boutique, signifying its grand opening. The drummer in the pit is so excited that he bursts out into a spontaneous tom roll.

ALL

WE'RE ASTOUNDED
JOEL YOU'VE FOUNDED
SOMETHING REALLY BLESSED
HERE'S TO LIVING
AND FORGIVING
LOVE AND HAPPINESS

BARBER TRIO AND BILL	PATRONS AND JOEL
GOOD MORNING MONDAY, MY FAVORITE TIME	GOOD MORNING MONDAY OH OH OH
THE PERFECT START TO A PERFECT WEEK	GOOD MORNING MONDAY AY
GOOD MORNING JOEL, IT'S YOUR TIME TO SHINE	GOOD MORNING MONDAY
AT JUDY'S FINE EVENINGWEAR BOUTIQUE, OH OH OH	

JOEL

GOOD MORNING BIRCHWOOD, IT LOOKS LIKE WE'VE GOT
THE START TO A BRAND NEW DAY
COME ON DOWN TO THIS NEW HOME OF MINE
YOU'D BETTER COME BY OUR WAY

ALL
YOU'D BETTER COME BY OUR WAY
YOU'D BETTER COME BY OUR WAY

> As the chorus parts and disseminate while the music rolls into its final chords, we see BUBBA stage center, exiting Judy's Fine Eveningwear Boutique wearing the dazzling suit he wore in the prologue. A snippet of the Barbershop Rag plays as he tips his hat.

ALL (CONT'D)
EVERYDAY!

> Blackout.
> The end.

ABOUT JACOB FJELDHEIM

Jacob Fjeldheim is an aspiring theatre composer and pianist in Gainesville, Florida. He spends most of his time vocally and musically directing plays at various playhouses and high schools, by no means the least of which being Eastside High School, where he had the privilege of putting on the first production of Barbershop Tales. This was his first full scale work, but certainly will not be his last.

He studies Mathematics and Physics and the University of Florida.

In the meantime, he plans to continue to write, listen, and learn at any possible opportunity.

ABOUT TYLER KERSTETTER

Tyler Kerstetter has somehow found himself living and working in beautiful Key West, Florida.

His free time is mostly split between spearfishing, playing rugby, and dreaming about his future travel plans. No matter what he's doing, though, he's always looking for inspiration for his next story.

He's written a number of short stories and is hoping to get more involved with longer pieces of prose. He's kind of banking on this creative thing to work out so he can travel freely.

For the time being he looks forward to working on more projects with his friends and enjoying the time God's given him.

ABOUT JACKSON SMITH

A writer currently based out of the Central Florida area, Jackson is honored to have worked with such talented and creative individuals on Barbershop Tales.

Recently graduated from the University of Central Florida with a degree in English, he has written for a thrice-weekly webcomic, worked on multiple student films, maintained and co-created a writing blog, in addition to working on many independently created short stories and scripts. However, Barbershop Tales has been one of the most ambitious projects he has been involved in yet, and though the process was long, he's ecstatic to see the work that the team put into this project finally come to life.

He thanks his family greatly for supporting his ventures and projects, no matter how strange they may sound, and he absolutely thanks the rest of the irreplaceable Corrupted Amish Productions team: Tyler Kerstetter, Jacob Fjeldheim, and Casey Doran, both for bringing him onto the team three years ago, and for allowing him the opportunity to turn a wonderfully silly idea into an actual performable production of musical theatre.

ABOUT CASEY DORAN

Casey Doran is a computer science student who resides in Merritt Island, Florida. When not spending most waking moments in the Gleason Performing Arts Center, he extensively studies software engineering, particularly quality assurance, education, testing, and security, at the Florida Institute of Technology.

He has thrice participated in the International Workshop on Teaching Software Testing and currently works for the Harris Institute for Assured Information doing computer security research. He hopes to design and build quality software in support of manned space exploration.

Casey is the titular character in "Black Hat, Grey: A Casey Doran Fanfiction" by Tyler Kerstetter and "Rick Scott's Worst Nightmare: A Casey Doran Fanfiction" by Jacob Fjeldheim, though rumors of his body count are greatly exaggerated.

This is the first work of fiction Casey has published, and he intends to put any proceeds towards eventually retiring on Mars.

Corrupted Amish Publishing

Plays and Musicals

Three Mile Smilin'

Tales of laughter, science, and sacrifice, straight from the reactor control room.

Where We Hid the Body

The hilarious tale of a heist gone horribly wrong, and the unlikely crooks who have to dispose of the corpse of a world champion sumo wrestler-turned-drug lord in the middle of a kitchenware convention.

Snowden: The Musical

When a lowly NSA employee uncovers what he believes to be the agency's deepest darkest secret only hilarity can ensue. Follow the misadventures of Edward Snowden, Vladimir Putin, Rafael Correa, and Barack Obama as one misinterpreted document gets blown way out of proportion!

Graphic Novels

The Adventures of Ronald Raygun

China, North Korea, and Russia have formed the Soviet League of Terrible Hideousness (or S.L.O.T.H) which has taken over much of the free world. Who will stand between S.L.O.T.H and world domination? Ronald Raygun, former President, newly minted cyborg.

Ronald Raygun: Red Scare

When a mysterious threat levels Paris, Ronald Raygun must save the world from his greatest threat yet: Robochev.

Ronald Raygun and the Prezobots

Sherman Truman (man from the waist up, tank from the waist down), Abe-robo-ham Lincoln (he'll emancipate your soul from your body), Tron F. Kennedy (how about a Bay of Exploding Pigs?) join Raygun to bring freedom to the world.

Down Right Radical

Join Regulus Stormdancer and Cid La Roc, two friends just trying to make their way in university full of mysterious dangers.

www.ingramcontent.com/pod-product-compliance
Lightning Source LLC
Chambersburg PA
CBHW020908090426
42736CB00008B/536